If Only I Had Listened

with Different Ears

Three Buddhist Tales

Written by Jason Siff

Introduction by Stephen Batchelor

Design: John Negru and Jason Siff
Cover art: Japanese scroll in Jason Siff's private collection
Jason Siff's portrait: David Douglas
Typeface: Athelas

Published by **The Sumeru Press Inc.**
PO Box 75, Manotick Main Post Office,
Manotick, ON, Canada K4M 0N5

LIBRARY AND ARCHIVES CANADA CATALOGUING IN PUBLICATION

Title: If only I had listened with different ears: Three Buddhist
  Tales / Jason Siff; introduction by Stephen Batchelor.
Names: Siff, Jason, author. 1958–
  Batchelor, Stephen, writer of introduction.
Identifiers: Canadiana 20210212314 |
ISBN 9781896559711 (softcover)
Subjects: LCGFT: Short stories.
Classification: LCC PS3619.I35 I3 2021 | DDC 813/.6—dc23

 For more information about Sumeru Books,
visit us at *sumeru-books.com*

CONTENTS

Introduction

The philosophers and ascetics of ancient India spent a lot of time walking alone or in small groups across the vast, flat plains of northern India, passing through scattered villages, stopping at the occasional town, resting in groves and shrines, then settling in parks to wait out the monsoon season before heading off again. These homeless mendicants belonged to a variety of religious traditions and were students of teachers with widely differing views. They would engage each other in conversation about their beliefs and practices, asking questions, challenging each other, in their struggle for understanding and truth. Kings, eager for knowledge themselves, would arrange public philosophical debates where people from all walks of life would encounter new, shocking ideas with open and wondering minds. Men and women alike were inspired to leave the familiar routines of domestic life to become itinerant monks and nuns in search of wisdom, often to their parents' incomprehension and despair. This is the world in which the three tales recounted in *If Only I Had Listened with Different Ears* take place.

These three tales—*King Bimbisara's Chronicler, After the Parinibbana,* and *Myth of Maitreya*—occur over a time span of roughly a thousand years (from the fifth century BCE to the fifth century CE). Some of the characters are historical figures, such as the Buddha, Mahavira (the founder of Jainism) and the brothers Asanga and Vasubandhu (both Buddhist philosophers), while two of the narrators, Padipa and Sujata, along with a few other characters, are entirely the author's creation. Each tale is self-contained but linked thematically to the others. The fabric of the book is woven from a number of recurring threads: the fragility of memory, the quest for enlightenment, the survival and evolution of ideas, and the tension between renunciation and life in the world. Yet despite being set in monasteries and hermitages, despite the monks and nuns who populate its pages, despite the passages quoted from Pali and Sanskrit texts, this is not a book about Buddhism. Whatever you may learn about Buddhism or other Indian religions is incidental to what drives and sustains the narrative. For like all literary fiction, these deceptively simple tales address the anguished question of what it means to be human.

As historical forms of Buddhism emerge into the daylight of globalized modernity, its teachers and practitioners seek a voice that can be heard outside the echo chamber of the faithful. This urge has nothing to do with persuading others of the truth of Buddhist beliefs or the efficacy of its practices. The ideas, doctrines, stories, myths, and imagery of the tradition are transformed into the raw materials of art. What the characters learn about themselves through overcoming the conflicts inherent in any dramatic narrative provides insights into their humanity rather than an endorsement of their faith. By serving as a resource for secular literature, the Buddhist religion takes a back seat to the refined, complex, and tragic sensibilities of men and women whose lives have been shaped by its practice.

Jason Siff possesses the rare gifts of a storyteller. His lyrical, unpretentious prose evokes a fully realized, consistent yet ever surprising world. With gentle, oblique irony he brings his characters to life, revealing their frailty and strengths, their joy and fear, their longings and disappointments. The rhythm and pacing of these tales are reminiscent of fables, while the quoted passages of ancient scripture evoke a distant past steeped in religious anguish and yearning. Yet the sympathy, care, and attention to detail with which Siff portrays his characters reveal them not as mythic or quasi-Biblical figures but as ordinary people struggling to make sense of their lives in an unambiguously human world.

To sustain this delicate balancing act between faithfulness to the textual sources of antiquity and the need for credible characters with whom a contemporary reader can identify is challenging. These tales inevitably recall Hesse's *Siddhartha* (1922), which is also set in northeast India during the Buddha's time. Yet unlike Hesse's famous work, which culminates in a generic mystical epiphany, the tales that Siff tells are fragmentary, tentative, and inconclusive. Siff's narrators Padipa, Sujata and Vasubandhu find themselves in proximity to sources of great wisdom, but continue to be unsure of themselves. The treasured memories that they transmit through their tales have clearly had a profound impact on them, but their voices lack the authority of the canonical scriptures they occasionally recite for inspiration. The seeming confidence with which they speak is belied by an undercurrent of uncertainty. For when sacred events and revered teachers are exposed to the gaze of contemporary fiction, a credible narrator is required to be tacitly conscious that his account is but one version of what actually happened.

Through paying keen attention to the impermanent, anguished, and contingent features of human experience, Buddhist practice may serve to deepen our sympathy with the characters and their dilemmas found in fictional narratives. Jason Siff's three tales are "Buddhist" in the sense that Nikos Kazantzakis', Graham Greene's, or Marilynne Robinson's novels are "Christian." These authors treat religious themes with great seriousness and offer compelling portraits of saints and priests, but do so from a consistently secular perspective. As Buddhism comes to terms with modernity, its practitioners too are bound to probe and mine the tradition imaginatively as part of the ongoing cultural conversation between Asia and the West. *If Only I Had Listened with Different Ears* presents figures from Buddhist history as characters in a distinctively European art form. In this way, readers of literary fiction are invited to inhabit the many-layered Buddhist worlds of ancient India, while Buddhist readers are invited to consider revered figures of their religion as fallible human beings like themselves.

Stephen Batchelor
Aquitaine, France, April 2021

King
Bimbisara's
Chronicler

Jason Siff

PROLOGUE

At the beginning of King Ajatasattu's reign

The seers say that the emperor's astrological chart is also the chart of the times. The houses of desire and wealth are strong in the birth chart of King Ajatasattu, while the houses of righteous action are weak, and those that speak of the king's spiritual progress are ruined.

King Ajatasattu imprisoned his father, King Bimbisara, and then barred anyone from bringing him food. I have heard the townspeople gossip about a natural succession of kings through patricide, as though the starving to death of our beloved King Bimbisara was a preordained sacrificial act. King Bimbisara, who ruled for over half a century, had reason and kindness to guide him through much of his long reign, and was not a murderous usurper to the throne of Magadha.

I feel like a traitor to my king, now that I work for his son, Ajatasattu, who has assigned me to chronicle the last days of the life of the sage, Nataputta. I have spent seven days with Nataputta, living with him and his sages in the barren hills southwest of Rajagaha. His followers say that in the years to come Nataputta will be revered as "Mahavira" (The Great Hero), founder of the Jain religion. To me he is just a *nigantha* (a naked ascetic), for that aptly describes what I see: a dirty, naked body, emaciated from fasting, a veritable feeding ground for lice and insects.

Yet here I am, chosen by my new king to acquire the teaching of this sage who seems to be nothing more than a misguided ascetic. I despise both of them, king and ascetic alike. How I yearn for the time when I was King Bimbisara's Chronicler and I sat beside Siddhattha Gotama, in the serenity of his presence, memorizing his wondrous teachings and stories. Why was I not sent to rejoin the Buddha and chronicle his teaching instead?

It is because of the powerful magic of the sage, Devadatta, a renegade member of the Buddha's Sangha and Siddhattha's own cousin. He has cast a spell of illusion over the mind of King Ajatasattu, turning him and his court against the Buddha and in favor of Nataputta. The demon, I hear, was even behind the plot to kill King Bimbisara.

If I could renounce my commission and quit this awful company, I would. But I am afraid of King Ajatasattu and Devadatta. They could imprison me, or worse yet, kill me, if I fail to bring them Nataputta's teaching.

What should I do now? I shall carry out my orders. Yet, all the while, I shall turn myself into a seer, a chronicler of history, recalling better days of thirty years ago, putting my mind on work which will eclipse the vicious actions of King Ajatasattu and Devadatta, and put Nataputta in his proper place as a confused, but earnest, ascetic.

May they be overlooked by history.

May our epoch be known as the age of the Buddha!

I

Thirty years earlier, during King Bimbisara's reign

I am Padipa. My father is Vipula, a distant relative of King Bimbisara and one of his ministers. My life before the age of twenty was that of a student. Only after passing many tests was I able to become one of the chroniclers of the court.

King Bimbisara first had me memorize three of his decrees word by word. Impressed by my flawless memory, the king gave me the task of listening to his public meetings. Every so often, he urged me to recount what others had said. Then one day two months later, King Bimbisara trusted me with an important mission. I was to find Siddhattha Gotama and memorize what he said to his disciples and to the public. The king assured me that I would be given an attendant for this undertaking and all my needs would be met. I bowed humbly before King Bimbisara and left happily on my search.

Where was I to find Siddhattha? First of all, people were calling him by several different names. Some called him, "The Buddha," others, "The Blessed One," and then there were those who called him, "The One Who Has Gone Thus." Whenever I asked someone the whereabouts of Siddhattha Gotama, there would be a moment of confusion over the proper name for the man I sought.

It was widely rumored that he wandered a great deal. How could he? He had injuries from his time as an ascetic. He had back pain, digestive troubles, and weakness in his muscles due to prolonged starvation. I thus assumed that the rumors of him staying at one place one day and then walking the whole day to another place were false. The most reasonable place to look for him would be at his cave beneath Vulture Peak, which lay not far from our beloved Rajagaha.

His cave had an arched entrance covered by a cloth. I walked inside without announcing myself. Inside the entrance was a twelve-year-old boy, with his hair cut short, wearing a brown cloth robe, which was draped across one shoulder and hung down to his feet.

The boy beckoned me to sit down on the bare floor of the cave. He smiled at me and offered to wash my feet. I declined his offer and then sat down cross-legged, waiting for Siddhattha to arrive.

I did not have to wait long for Siddhattha. He entered with his alms bowl in hand. He had already eaten and disposed of his leftovers. He immediately went over to a table where he carefully placed his black-lacquered iron alms bowl on a cloth, making sure that it would remain upright. He turned around and noticed me sitting on the hard cold floor of his cave.

I stood up and introduced myself with my hands clasped in a greeting. He returned my greeting in kind, and then motioned me to be seated.

Siddhattha was not a terribly big man. He was slightly taller than average, slim, with a round, pleasant looking face and almond-colored skin. At forty he looked healthy, although I could detect a grayness, a coarseness of once fine features beginning to take over. I found myself contrasting my appearance with his. We were about the same height, build, and weight. My face was narrower, my nose squashed in a bit, just enough to make me feel that a beautiful woman would never fall in love with me. Siddhattha, on the other hand, was said to have wed one of the most beautiful women in the world before he renounced his worldly inheritance and became a sage.

"I am here," I said, "to carry your teaching to King Bimbisara."

"I am honored that our king finds value in my words. I do not expect you or him to truly understand me," Siddhattha said. "The delight of full liberation of mind is inexpressible in conventional terms. You may recount my words, but you cannot recount the final ceasing of anguish and desire.

"You must have a good memory for the king of Magadha to trust you to faithfully relay the teaching of the Buddha. That may be your path, the path of recollecting all the wisdom you have heard, studying it, analyzing it, until one day you realize for yourself the highest peace. You may forget, however, so much of what I say that you will think it is not there, that you cannot do it. Then, in a moment of penetrating recollection, you will see for yourself that all these lives are woven out of the same fabric. You untie the knot and all you are left with is a heap of threads."

I did not expect him to address me personally. It felt uncomfortable to use my excellent memory to remember something about myself. I feared that Siddhattha's addressing me personally, if it were to become known, would make me appear to the royal court as a servant who only thinks of himself.

Siddhattha said, "In the practice of recollective awareness, there are four fields. One is the body. Two is the knowledge of life. Three is where the mind has been. Four is the teaching of what is true.

"One recollects the body in all of its postures and how it looks when diseased and at death, knowing how attachment forms for its pleasures and hatred forms for its pains. One dwells in this body seeing the hunger for rebirth for what it is, not taking it up as the aim and purpose of life.

"One recollects the knowledge of life, that life is pleasant and painful, and neither pleasant nor painful. One recalls where the mind has been, that it has been with lust, hatred, confusion, dullness, distractedness; and that it has also been exalted, been liberated, been stilled, been at peace. Finally, one thoroughly recollects the teaching of what is true, learning about the obstacles to knowledge and what true knowledge is."

Keeping up with his speech and committing it to memory was easy. I was not familiar with the precise meaning of some of his words, but I think I understood what he was saying. I suppose that if I had been able to ask Siddhattha to clarify what he meant, I would have been able to fully comprehend it. But at that exact moment, a group of young men entered Siddhattha's cave.

Even though the light was dim, I could discern that all five of them were noblemen. They wore fine silk garments. They hesitated before sitting down in the center of the cave, near the Buddha, unsure about what to do when no cushions were offered. One of them took out a piece of cloth and placed it on the ground. He then plopped down on it, rolling off to his left before righting himself. The other four laughed, joyfully pulling out pieces of cloth and laying them on the ground, sitting down more ceremoniously than the first fellow. I moved closer to the Buddha, sitting on his right between him and the others, where I could hear everything they said.

Siddhattha seemed to know who they were without having met them before, for he said, "Welcome princes from the Licchavi clan. I am honored by your presence."

"Venerable Sage," one of them said, "we listened to your teaching as expounded by your *bhikkhus* residing in Vesali, the city of our ancestors. We developed a thirst for your *Dhamma,* and they told us that we could have an audience with you in Rajagaha. We have come all this way to ask you some questions about how to live one's life to the peak of perfection and happiness."

Siddhattha said, "My way may not agree with you."

Another man replied, "We are prepared to change our lives. Even though we have wealth and status, enjoying the best this world has to offer, we are not entirely happy. I am sad much of the time. Little things disturb me. I have too many thoughts and my heart does not obey me. What birth has given me as the way to happiness and perfection seems full of sorrow."

I was stunned to hear a Licchavi prince speak this way. What an ingrate! How disrespectful to his father, his clan, his ancestors! As the brahmins tell us, we are what we are by birth, and it is our duty to fulfill the work of our station. In that way we may be reborn in better circumstance than we now enjoy.

"Young Prince," Siddhattha said, "you have the knowledge of life, that it is painful and pleasant, but you do not have the liberating knowledge. You know the ailment and not the cure. The teaching is like a skilled healer and it is also not like a skilled healer. A skilled healer knows the name of the affliction, its course, and the herbs and spells to treat it. The Dhamma knows no herbs nor spells. There is no right diet, except to moderate and examine your desires. There is no medicine, except the words of those who have crossed the sea of suffering and reached the pinnacle of inner peace. There are no dressings for wounds, except the deeper and exalted states of meditation. There is only one cure: quenching the thirst for one existence after another."

"Tell us, Siddhattha, Sage of the Sakyas," the second man said, "what is the way that leads to quenching?"

"It is neither this nor that, but thus."

Siddhattha then folded his hands in his lap, closed his eyes, and vanished within himself.

II

With Siddhattha meditating, there was nothing for me to memorize. I was of no use right then, so I stood up and silently made my way out. Once outside, I was blinded by the brightness of the sunlight as it reflected off the rocks. I felt a little dizzy, as if I had drunk a cup of palm wine.

I walked back to Rajagaha and got a room at an inn. I had decided not to sleep at my father's house for the duration of this mission. The thought of staying with my family felt burdensome. I believed that I needed freedom from my other chores and responsibilities in order to concentrate fully on the task at hand. I told the innkeeper that I would stay as long as Siddhattha was at Vulture Peak. Once Siddhattha left, I was to accompany him.

The innkeeper said, "So many men like you are following Siddhattha these days, and some of them end up as beggars in the street."

I said, "I do not plan on becoming a follower, but, if you must know, I am a relative of King Bimbisara, and being one of his primary chroniclers, he assigned me to memorize the words of Siddhattha Gotama. On occasion, I will be reciting the verses I intend to compose from Siddhattha's teachings."

"Good," he said, "then I won't be bothering you as long as you are paid up."

"Good," I said, and went up to my room to sleep.

I slept deeply and woke up to the voices of men talking in the street outside my window. From the hue of the light streaming into my room, I initially thought that it was dawn and I had slept the whole night through, but it was actually sunset. When I looked out my window, I was stunned to see about twenty men dressed in colorful silks.

Scurrying out of bed, I quickly dressed in my finest robe. I wanted to appear to these men to be of a station where I could address them and not be dismissed.

I ran downstairs, but when I arrived at the front door, the innkeeper grabbed me by the shoulders. He whispered in my ear, "These men are trying to find out where Siddhattha is staying. They are looking for their young princes. You must warn Siddhattha."

I looked into his eyes and saw his fear. Then I left through the back door.

The moon was rising in the exact direction of the hills. I was able to find the footpath leading to Vulture Peak. No one followed me. I was sure of that, since I stopped to look behind me a few times. At the edge of the grove, I heard some voices coming from deep within it, which sounded like the chanting of brahmin priests. Walking in the direction of the solemn voices brought me to a clearing that was illuminated by firebrands. I could see several of Siddhattha's bhikkhus in their long brown robes congregated around him. I pushed through the outer layers of the crowd until I reached a place where I could see all that was going on.

Siddhattha was in the center with two bhikkhus beside him, both of whom were chanting verses. In front of Siddhattha were five men, who knelt with their newly shaved heads bowed low. I surmised that this was an ordination ceremony.

The chanting stopped. Then Siddhattha spoke to the men kneeling before him. His clear, calm voice filled the grove.

"From this day on, you will not own land or jewels, nor will you use money. You may only live in caves, underneath trees, in abandoned huts, or in modest lodgings given to bhikkhus by lay supporters. You will speak the truth. You will not take what is not freely given. You will not kill nor harm other sentient beings, and you will not marry nor lie with women. These are the essential precepts of the bhikkhu's life. Honor them, learn them, practice them, and your search for complete liberation from the wheel of birth and death will be that much more certain, though not absolutely certain.

"Liberation of mind can be attained in many ways. The sage who does not shave his head, nor live in the open, nor practice fully the higher precepts can still arrive at liberation, though his mind may be distracted by desires and their fulfillment. Still, let it be known that those who remain in the world can still arrive at

JASON SIFF ❋ 19

the path to liberation and follow it diligently. Do you still decide to go forth as a shaven-headed bhikkhu?"

One of the men looked up at Siddhattha with sadness in his eyes, his body trembling. Siddhattha peered into his eyes, smiled, and nodded his head as if to say, "Young Prince, it is all right to return to the life you have decided to leave."

The man stood up, bowed to Siddhattha, and walked away. The four other former princes took side glances at each other, but not one of them got up to leave.

Looking at the four remaining men, Siddhattha said, "Please tell us why you have decided to become a bhikkhu."

I recognized the first to speak as the second prince who spoke up that morning, the one who expressed ingratitude for the noble life he was born into. He stood up straight and turned to face the crowd. There was a fire of determination in his eyes. His voice was strong and smooth, though his bearing was mild.

He said, "Before today, my life was going to be as my father had planned. As a king, I would have had the wealth and power to do whatever I pleased. But I would have been bound by the servitude of my birth, never light, nor free, nor at peace. Therefore, I go forth in the teaching of Siddhattha, where wisdom arises in the freedom from sorrow. I shall from this day on walk in Siddhattha's shadow to Siddhattha's light."

These were thrilling words, and in my absorption of feeling, I could not remember a single phrase immediately afterward. It was as though I had forgotten who I was for a few moments. Or did I forget what the former prince had said because a commotion ensued? Just after he had finished, a group of men entered the clearing, speaking loudly and angrily, pushing me and others aside as they made their way through the crowd.

III

I was more concerned about dirt getting on my finest robe than in what was happening around me. As I got to my feet and inspected my robe, brushing it off in places, I was aware that the multitude of voices had died down and there were now only two voices. I recognized one voice as Siddhattha's, who spoke softly, unaffected by the commotion. The other voice belonged to a man about the same age as Siddhattha. I later learned that he was a minister to the Licchavi king, Chetaka. His name was Ghosa, "He Who Shouts," on account of his booming voice.

Ghosa spoke in reply to something that Siddhattha said, which I missed because I was fussing with my robe.

"King Chetaka, the father of this young prince who just spoke with such conviction, is sad and miserable on account of his son's absence. If you take his son into your Sangha, King Chetaka will surely not rise from his anguish. It is said that you do not teach in order to cause suffering, but to free people from it. So why does your teaching cause our king so much grief?"

Siddhattha replied, "I have not caused this grief you speak of. All sadness, all arguments, all conflict between people, and all slander and lies have their source in holding things dear to one's heart. It is because King Chetaka holds his son as dear to his heart as his own life that he suffers so."

"Siddhattha, is there anything wrong in a father holding his son as dear to him as his own life? How else should it be?"

Siddhattha paused for a moment. I assumed that he would give in and allow the former prince to return to his grieving father.

But instead, Siddhattha said, "There is taking pleasure in his son, at his appearance, skill, and accomplishments, which causes grief and anguish when he believes he has lost his son. It could not be otherwise for someone who has not arrived at full liberation of mind."

"Why then," Ghosa said, "when you know King Chetaka has not arrived at full liberation of mind, do you take his son from him and cause him to feel unrelenting anguish?"

"King Chetaka has not seen the attainment of the highest inner peace and end of suffering known by his son. For if he had, he would not grieve this loss. He would rejoice at his son's attainment. Tell King Chetaka that his son is an *arahant*. If he would like to see this for himself, let him invite his son, along with me and my bhikkhus, to his palace in Vesali."

Then Ghosa spoke with a fierceness I was not accustomed to, for King Bimbisara always spoke in a gentle voice, as did most of his subjects.

"Siddhattha, if you are attempting to deceive me with a tale, let the hell realms take you when it is your time. I will relay your message to King Chetaka. If he then wishes to see his son, you will be invited to Vesali. Though I doubt he will be able to tolerate seeing his son dressed in a robe made out of rags."

Ghosa turned to speak to his men, ordering them to return to their kingdom and tell King Chetaka what they had witnessed. As the Licchavi countrymen left in the direction of Rajagaha, the bhikkhus walked in the opposite direction toward Vulture Peak. I stood there in the clearing alone with Siddhattha. He then spoke to me.

"What do you say, Chronicler? Do I make up tales about arahants, or do I truly see and know?"

This question frightened me, for I was divided within. I said, "How could I ever judge what you see and know?"

"You speak like one who holds no views so as to gain favor. Such speech does not purify the mind. Instead, it gives others a false impression of you while you keep your true convictions hidden. It is better to say that I lie if that is what you believe. Such speech cannot harm you."

"Then, Venerable Siddhattha," I said, "I believe you deceived and tricked Ghosa. It seemed convenient to make the Licchavi Crown Prince into an arahant. It suited your purpose."

"Well reasoned," Siddhattha said. "Then consider this: Would I risk my reputation and the validity of my teaching just to settle a dispute in my favor?"

"Siddhattha," I said, growing braver each moment, "I do not know you well enough to say what you would do when you are engaged in a dispute with another person. My knowledge of human nature tells me that people use lies, slander, and clever reasoning when there is no other way to win a dispute."

Siddhattha said, "Perhaps you need to know me better."

And I replied, "Perhaps I do."

"Then join me tomorrow, the next day, and each day thereafter until it is time for us to part ways."

Siddhattha's face shone brightly in the moonlight. A tender wave of compassion curled around my heart and I felt certain that spending time with Siddhattha, memorizing his words for King Bimbisara, could do me no harm.

IV

Spending each day with Siddhattha was never dull. At first, I tried to understand what he was like as a person.

In the area of character, he was an enigma. He had great confidence in his teaching. He would speak at length about what liberation of mind did for those who arrived at it, but I could not tell who arrived at it or not. Neither could some of his bhikkhus. Every so often, one of his bhikkhus would approach him to ask if another bhikkhu had arrived at complete liberation of mind. Sometimes the bhikkhu asking the question was sent to Siddhattha by the other bhikkhu, who wanted to get the Buddha's superior insight on whether he had attained liberation or not. But most often it was a legitimate concern of one bhikkhu wishing to know if one of his friends had made it to the end and what that end may then look like. The way Siddhattha would say, "Yes, he has truly seen the end of all longing and knows the stilling of mind only attained by arahants," about one person and then say, "No, he prides himself on an attainment he does not have," about another person made me wonder how he could know these things for sure. Was he just making all this up as he went along?

When people felt this doubt as I did, they would ask Siddhattha to explain the qualities of an arahant. Hearing Siddhattha enumerate the virtues and spiritual accomplishments of arahants did not vanquish my doubt. On the contrary, it gave me new reasons to be skeptical of ordinary men becoming arahants.

One day, the Buddha spoke to a group of bhikkhus about doubt. He said, "Doubt can only be overcome by arriving at *nibbana*. The fully liberated mind no longer experiences doubt.

Until that time, one needs to trust the Buddha, the Dhamma, and the Sangha in order to arrive at the path to nibbana."

I then asked him the question that was foremost on my mind for many days, "If I doubt you, then is it impossible for me to arrive at nibbana?"

Siddhattha said, "You have not even begun the journey when this doubt so dominates your consciousness. As a worldly person, you wonder if I am a fraud, not seeing that I am a good friend. Even though you listen to my words and try to comprehend my teaching, you are still not on the path to nibbana."

His bluntness offended me, stinging deep within my chest. It was during moments like these that I understood how there were people who hated Siddhattha and spread vicious rumors about him. These feelings would slowly fade away as I remained in his presence. When he smiled at me with his profound compassion, I felt the sting evaporate and the hole in my heart mend. Then he would say something that would sting, and I would be stirred up again.

In this emotional climate, it was hard to concentrate solely on the task of memorizing. I did it conscientiously, but all the while I was beginning to see how divided and conflicted my heart was inside. I wanted both to return to King Bimbisara before exposing myself to more of the Buddha's teaching and to spend every waking moment with Siddhattha and memorize everything he said. I revered his infinite wisdom, yet I disdained his penetrating vision into the souls of others, especially my own.

Then there were times I would feel a yearning to arrive at nibbana, only so that I could say to him, "Now I know what this is all about!" I would then imagine Siddhattha praising me and telling everyone to rejoice as he had done for others in my presence.

Each night before bed, I would go over the fundamental beliefs I held about the true purpose and meaning of my existence. This went completely against the Buddha's teaching, but I did it anyhow. I had to. It was about survival, about being myself. I repeated in my mind: I am an accomplished chronicler in the service of King Bimbisara. I will get married and raise a family.

I will bring honor to my parents and leave a great name for my children and future generations.

In doing this, I kept both my soul and my sacred task intact.

V

Two weeks had passed since the ordination of the Licchavi princes. The incident had faded from my memory and was not discussed among the bhikkhus residing at Vulture Peak. Then a messenger arrived from King Chetaka to invite the Buddha and the former princes to come to the city of Vesali. Siddhattha was pleased by this invitation and announced that he intended to go. Some of the elder bhikkhus objected to his traveling, concerned as they were about his health. He assured them that he would be alive for many more years and they should let him do the work he was meant to do. It was decided that we would leave the next day.

I could have taken this opportunity to report back to King Bimbisara, but I decided not to. I had a plan to condense the Buddha's teaching into verse and had already composed the opening stanzas. When I finished composing the poem, I would then consider my assignment to be done. Then I would present it to King Bimbisara as the essence of the Buddha's Dhamma.

I structured the poem in a traditional form used for religious discourse. The person speaking in first stanza is the questioner, namely someone like me, who is filled with doubts. In the second stanza, the Buddha imparts his superior wisdom.

From what source do arguments,
Disputes, sorrow, and envy arise?
Tell me about the source of pride,
Self-importance, and slander?

From holding something dear comes pride,
Arguments, disputes, sorrow, and envy.
Envy is connected with arguments and disputes,
While arguments give birth to slanderous words.

VI

King Bimbisara offered Siddhattha horses and elephants to make this long journey, but Siddhattha declined. We were going to walk. That being so, I planned on having my attendant carry my belongings.

I needed more time to prepare than the single day Siddhattha gave me. This was a day of anger, worry, and lust. I was thrown off balance by the power of these emotions. During those weeks with Siddhattha, my mind had been mostly tranquil and collected, and even those moments of hurt and doubt were mild compared to the storm of agitation that was unleashed within me as I prepared for this journey.

My attendant was an older man by the name of Drona, who had been the personal attendant of one of our chief ministers for twenty years. He had been removed from that esteemed position on account of his drinking and gambling. Like many of those who drink intoxicating beverages, he was lazy and never around when I needed him. He loved to tell bawdy jokes and fantastic tales. What he thought of me was not flattering. I heard a rumor that he took me for being a weak, insignificant, easily manipulated boy. Perhaps he was right.

He was nowhere to be found when I heard we were to be leaving the next day. The precious little time I had to collect my belongings for the journey was taken up looking for him. He was harder to find than Siddhattha was that first day, perhaps because there are any number of places for lowlifes to frequent. I searched the drinking places, the gambling places, the neighborhoods of prostitutes, but could not find him anywhere.

That evening, worn out by my search, I went to my room at the inn, packed a small bag of clothes and paid the innkeeper to send my remaining possessions to my father's house.

I was awakened in the middle of the night by a loud banging on my door. It was Drona. He had heard that I was looking for him. He had also heard, before I had, that Siddhattha was leaving the next day, and so had taken the opportunity to visit a mistress of his in a nearby village.

"I had to see my mistress once more before our long journey," he said, "if you know what I mean?"

"I don't!" I said. I was furious but polite.

Drona took off his upper robe, baring his flabby chest. He sat down on my bed, right next to me. I could smell the alcohol coming out of his pores, his breath, his stinking feet. To make this even more odious, he began to lecture me.

"You do not realize what you would miss, but I sure knew what I would be missing going off with a bunch of gentlemen masquerading as sages. They are liars and cheats more dishonest than highway robbers. Thieves should dress and act like thieves, not holy men, not beggars, not disgruntled noblemen in white cotton and silks. They come through a village in large groups and are put up in the apartments of wealthy nobles and kings, eating and drinking their fill, the envy of all the toiling villagers, robbing the town of its stored grains and cloth and (here he burped loudly) rice alcohol. I have seen it with my own eyes in Savatthi, where a group of wandering sages were entertained by King Pasenadi for many days, leaving with gold, jewels, and several cartloads of food and cloth, as the townspeople wept bitterly and cursed their foolish king."

Drona then began to cough heavily, giving me a chance to interject, "It is late and I must get some sleep."

"You have not been listening!"

"Yes, I have!" I said. "It is all a tall tale that you have made up to persuade me to stay here, so that you can drink and gamble."

"You are a fool!"

Drona then stood up and stomped off, slamming the door with a rattle that echoed as he descended the wooden stairs to the lobby. I thought I would be rid of him till morning. But no. He came back a few minutes later, just as I was drifting off to sleep.

Drona dragged a woman with him as he entered my room. He held a lantern up to her face. I could see she was young and pretty, with long black hair. He grabbed her left arm, squeezing her flesh as he led her to my bed.

"Young Master," he said, "here is a woman for you, free of charge. Just remember the favor."

He threw her toward me as I sat upright in bed. Her body fell across my legs. She grunted once and then let out a muffled yell, so soft and yet so violent. Drona stomped out of the room and slammed the door.

I pulled my legs out from underneath the woman and scurried out of bed. I customarily wore only a thin under-robe when I went to sleep, so I had to put on a full robe before leaving my room. My mind swam in a sea of rage, making it difficult for me to stay focused on anything other than finding Drona and putting him in his place as my attendant. I ran downstairs to the lobby. It was empty. I went outside. He was nowhere to be seen.

I walked down the street to where an old woman sat hunched over. I touched her shoulder to see if she was awake. Her eyes opened instantly.

"Did you see a man walk by here a moment ago?"

She said, "Why follow him and question me when a maiden awaits you in your bed?"

"You — !" I yelled, boiling with indignation. This woman should be imprisoned and tortured for what she does! Suddenly, I became aware of the strength of my emotions. I stood perfectly still, feeling the hatred surging through my body. It intensified briefly, like a fire doused with oil, and then it extinguished itself like a candle flame blown out by the wind.

Still, I was firm with the old woman.

"I will not have her! I'm sending her back to you."

She replied, "You will still owe me five *kahapanas* and will have gotten nothing in return. You are a fool. Enjoy her. You have till sunrise."

I became less angry at the old woman as I resigned myself to accepting the girl for the night. Then some other emotion took hold of me, a kind of confusion, or agitation, for I realized that I was presented with a moral dilemma before the journey tomorrow. How would I be able to look Siddhattha in the eye from having delighted in the sexual embraces of a prostitute?

"I will have her," I said.

"My five kahapanas," she said, holding out a palm crimped with lines and crevices.

"Drona paid for her!" I yelled uncontrollably. I then glanced at the windows and doorways up and down the street to see if anyone heard my outburst.

She said, in a menacing tone, "You fool, Drona never pays. He just takes what he wants. Pay up or I will have my men after you in the morning."

What are five kahapanas to me? It is surely wiser to pay now than be beaten up in the morning.

I unfurled my money cloth, which luckily had been tied to my under-robe as I had often feared that I would be robbed in my sleep while staying at the inn. I gave her five kahapana coins, all that I had.

I walked back to the inn, imagining losing my virginity and how delightful that would be. That train of thought abruptly stopped when I suddenly recalled hearing Siddhattha say that arahants have eliminated sexual desire. For a moment, I became curious about what it would be like not to experience lust for a woman's body, but then concluded that such an attainment was beyond my comprehension.

I opened the door to my room slowly. It was dark inside, except for a small oil lamp on a table near my bed. I picked up the lamp and edged closer to my bed, leaning over it to see the woman who was supposed to be in it. She was there all right. Moving the lamp to illuminate more of the room, I saw her clothes placed in a tiny, neat pile on the floor near the bed. I stood over her naked body, asleep underneath a diaphanous bed sheet, listening to her soft breathing for what seemed like an eternity.

VII

Thirty years later, during King Ajatasattu's reign

Another seven days have passed in the company of Nataputta. He has been observing a vow of silence, fasting all the while. Since he has not spoken to me even once, my time has been spent recollecting those first few weeks with Siddhattha.

Nothing about this place is pleasant. It is cold at night and hot during the day. The nigantha sages live without clothing and shelter on a rocky hillside. The hill faces a deserted valley, offering no distraction. For without pleasurable things, they believe, one will cut ties with the world. I miss Siddhattha's wise perspective on these matters. For him, sitting in the shade next to a forest stream on a hot day, listening to the birdsong, feeling a cool mountain breeze brush across your skin were all woven into being liberated in the here and now.

A messenger from Rajagaha delivered some bad news earlier today. My father has taken ill and my brother fears that he may die soon. I sent the messenger back to my brother to tell him that I will be returning to Rajagaha later today.

Unfortunately, because of Nataputta's vow of silence over these past two weeks, I have nothing to report to King Ajatasattu. Maybe I will just have to make something up. He will never be the wiser, though Devadatta might find out through some devious questioning or the use of his psychic powers. Perhaps I should not take the risk. I think I can get one of the other niganthas who is not following the vow of silence to recount something Nataputta has said before. Who can I approach?

I look around at the six niganthas, standing or sitting in contorted postures, all of them naked. The nigantha, Tapassi, standing on a large boulder, facing the sun, catches my attention. This nigantha elder engaged Siddhattha in a debate a few years ago and lost. Since he has often preached the doctrine of the Jains, perhaps he will be willing to speak to me.

"Tapassi," I shout to him, "I seek to know your Master's teaching, so that King Ajatasattu may benefit from it and grow in sainthood."

He turns around and looks down, blinking his eyes in an attempt to see in my direction. It takes him a few moments to focus on my form.

"Oh, it is you, Chronicler," Tapassi says. "What would King Ajatasattu need to know for his progress toward sainthood?"

"The king would want to know what Nataputta says about acquiring good fortune and success?"

"Nataputta instructs his disciples to renounce all worldly possessions, cares, and thoughts."

"Good, I see he is wise to the snares of the world," I say, while thinking to myself that he is not wise to the snares of asceticism.

Tapassi says, "A nigantha sage does not possess desire for good fortune nor aversion to misfortune. All outcomes are the same to him. Success, no success, there is no difference. The enlightened mind is unaffected by what goes on in the world."

"All things being equal," I ask, "what is the use of good actions in the world?"

"A good action always involves self-restraint. Only then can the unwholesome *kamma* that clings to the soul be cleansed."

Confident in my reasoning ability, I say, "So, if I understand what you are saying, and infer what you do not say directly, then you believe that a good deed, such as being a wise and good friend, is not a good action because it does not involve restraint."

Without taking a moment to consider his reply, Tapassi says, "If it is done while restraining the senses and not creating kamma, then yes, it can be a good action. The best action is taking the vows of a nigantha and doing only those ascetic practices that lead to the soul's liberation."

"I understand your teaching and have memorized its points. May I present your words to King Ajatasattu as Nataputta's teaching, as told to me by his revered disciple, Tapassi?"

"You may."

Tapassi returns to standing on a rock, facing the sun, and, I guess, cleansing his soul of the residue from past kamma.

As I walk back to Rajagaha, my thoughts do not go toward my father's illness, but rather pursue a recollection of the days I spent with Siddhattha and his bhikkhus on our journey to Vesali.

VIII

Thirty years earlier, during King Bimbisara's reign

I awoke to the sound of my name being called out in a boy's high-pitched voice, "Padipa! Padipa!" I turned over in bed and was surprised that the young woman had left sometime in the early morning without my noticing. I quickly dressed and collected my bundle of clothes, neglecting to wash up. I ran down the stairs and out the door, anxious that I might be left behind. The boy was outside waiting for me. He was the same young monk, a *samanera*, I had seen in Siddhattha's cave.

We hurried through town toward the northern gate of the city, where the road to the Ganges began. King Bimbisara had ordered the road smoothed out and decorated with colorful banners for the Buddha's journey to Vesali. He also had his builders erect some rest houses along the way, and we were to stop at a new one each night.

Once through the gate, off in the distance, I could see a long line of brown-robed bhikkhus with the occasional layman wearing white interspersed among them. The samanera and I ran as fast as we could to join them. I felt so elated seeing the bhikkhus walking behind Siddhattha in the distance that I had completely forgotten about the woman I was with last night and my despicable attendant. But as soon as I caught up with the train of bhikkhus, I felt shame arise within me and obliterate the joy I had previously known. I could not face Siddhattha just then. My pace slowed down and I found a spot near the end of the procession, some fifty people behind Siddhattha.

As I walked in the warm morning sun, never straying from the line of people in front of me, I noticed how each footstep was different. When my mind wandered from the movement of my feet, it went to angry thoughts about my attendant and to shame over my lapse of judgment with the woman. I became preoccupied with my fear of Siddhattha's reaction during these short mind-wanderings. But then I came back to the impact of my feet touching the sandy ground, at the end of a line of bhikkhus, walking in the morning sun on a glorious spring day.

We stopped at a giant banyan tree to partake of the lone meal of the day. The elder bhikkhus sat down in the shade, while the younger bhikkhus and samaneras began unpacking food and jugs of water. There was a breeze jangling the green leaves of the tree, throwing off darts of light that landed on the shaven heads and newly washed robes of the elders.

I paced back and forth around the outer rim of the banyan tree, experimenting with the new awareness of walking that I had discovered. Little did I know that Siddhattha would also pace back and forth like this, his mind focused on the movement of his legs and the impact of his feet, while also knowing the freshness of each moment, whether it be a moment of vision, of sound, of smell, or of the mind a little distant, floating in the air like a kite on a string.

My concentration was broken by the samanera. He walked up to me and stared at me, waiting for me to stop my pacing and give him my full attention. A moment later I did.

"Siddhattha requests the chronicler to join him for the morning meal," he said, full of respect for me.

"I have my own food," I said.

He implored a second time, "Please join Siddhattha."

I did not want to argue a point for which I held no conviction, for I was truly hungry and wanted to be with Siddhattha no matter how much remorse I might feel in his presence. So I followed the samanera over toward the trunk of the banyan tree and sat down next to Siddhattha. He greeted me with a friendly smile. A man dressed in white knelt down and placed a leaf in my hands. I looked into the leaf and saw cooked rice with lentils. With my right hand I made a ball out of the rice and lentils, slowly lifting it to my mouth. I noticed how it felt on my tongue, then how it tasted as I chewed, feeling the food go down my throat and into my belly. It was the most delicious meal of my life. I did not know what was happening to me, but it was profound. My shame did not return to haunt me. My anger at my attendant dissolved completely. It felt as though existence began and ended where I sat. There was no going into the past nor the future. Time was held in the arising and perishing of each impression, each thought, each union of the enjoyer and the enjoyed.

Then the thought arose that this must be liberation.

I said nothing. I sat quietly and finished my food. When I was done, I got up and bowed to Siddhattha. He looked me in the eye, and I knew a special kind of fear. My secret pride was visible. I could see it reflected in his tranquil brown eyes. No words passed between us. I walked away knowing that I had deceived myself.

But how had that happened? I had honestly understood the truths of impermanence and emptiness. Most decisively of all, I had experienced my mind being liberated in the momentary stopping of time. From that time on, I could no longer fully trust my own judgments on what I experienced, and so a new aspect was added to my already existing doubts.

IX

We reached the first rest house a little after midday and spent the remainder of the day resting and meditating. Then toward nightfall, one of the bhikkhus informed me that the Buddha was about to speak to a wandering ascetic who had come from Baranasi to meet him.

Siddhattha sat cross-legged on top of a small boulder. His bhikkhus sat on the ground in a circle, many of them with eyes closed in meditation. An emaciated old man dressed only in a loincloth stood in front of the Buddha.

I found a place to sit on the Buddha's left, where I could hear everything.

The ascetic said, "I have heard that Siddhattha Gotama, who is revered as the Buddha of this age, makes known a teaching based on his own realization and not that of others. It is said that Siddhattha attains exalted states of consciousness to abandon the desire for them, and not for the enjoyment of exalted states. I am curious about this teaching, for I enjoy exalted states and through them experience the abandonment of worldly desire and attachment. What is the harm that the Buddha sees in enjoying exalted states of consciousness?"

Siddhattha remained silent for some time before answering. It appeared as though he were considering every angle of the question. At that time, I imagined him to be far more calculating than he really was. I could not fathom someone considering his responses for so long without attributing some base motive. Later on, I understood that he just wanted to be careful about everything he said, for he knew that people would make more than he could ever mean out of his every utterance.

Finally, Siddhattha said, "All exalted states are like delicious food. Without the ingredients, the pot, the fire, and the cook, they do not exist. When fine food is enjoyed, attachment and desire also arise for the ingredients, the pot, the fire, and the cook, not just the food. Just so, exalted states require the appropriate mental and physical conditions. When these conditions are enjoyed, attachment and desire form for rebirth in the realm of the gods, and one seeks to attain the consciousness of Brahma. When those conditions are not enjoyed, there is no desire for celestial rebirth, and the arahant knows that he has passed beyond the consciousness of Brahma, where he can no longer experience the sorrows of existence."

Siddhattha paused a few moments to let his words echo in his listeners' ears before addressing another aspect of the ascetic's question.

"Whenever there is a trace of one kind of desire, there is the existence of all three kinds of desire. That is, when there is the desire for celestial rebirth, the desire for worldly pleasures also exists in one. When there is the desire for non-existence, the desire for celestial rebirth also exists in one. The desire for worldly pleasures, for celestial rebirth, and for non-existence all have their source in one's knowledge of life coming from ignorance. Knowing that life is painful and pleasant, and neither painful nor pleasant, is ignorance when that knowledge comes from what has been heard from others and not realized within oneself. It is ignorance when it comes from unquestioning adherence to tradition. It is ignorance when it comes from intellectual theories and speculation. It is ignorance when it denies the efficacy and power of wise intentions and good actions. It is ignorance when there is pride, arrogance, envy, and ill-will in the heart. The Wise Ones know life in each and every possible realm of existence as being driven by desire and ending in sorrow.

Who then would take up any existence and say, 'May I have this life for eternity?'"

The old ascetic listened attentively to everything Siddhattha said. He indicated neither approval nor disapproval as Siddhattha spoke. But then, after a few moments of silence, I noticed his cheeks redden and a teardrop form under his right eye.

He said, "I am old and near the end of this life. If I abandon my hope of rebirth in the realm of the gods, then my life will have been wasted, and I will be filled with remorse and dread. Not to have a celestial rebirth is the worst kind of pain I can possibly know. Please, Siddhattha, tell me how I can remove this anguish, for I now feel without hope in the face of approaching death."

Siddhattha responded without a second thought this time, standing up on the boulder to address the whole assembly.

"Let the arahants gathered here instruct you on the path to final liberation. Apply yourself to the practices they teach and you will find the end of remorse and dread."

Saying this, he got down from the boulder and walked toward his hut.

X

I rose from my seat and followed Siddhattha. My shame from having been with a prostitute the night before returned during Siddhattha's discourse to the ascetic. It pained me to see how low and common my desires really were, as I had not the least bit interest in a celestial rebirth and the idea of non-existence as a desirable condition never entered my mind.

Just outside his hut, Siddhattha turned around, having become aware that I was behind him.

He asked, "What troubles you, Padipa?"

"I have remorse and shame over a past action."

"Was the action something you wanted to perform, or were you forced to do it by someone else?"

"It was both, but mostly it was something I wanted."

"Then," Siddhattha said, "you have known the suffering that follows upon a desire being fulfilled, whereby new remorse and longings are born. As long as you are attentive to the truth of desire, its fulfillment, and its fruits, you will have no need for remorse and shame. For you will have awareness instead. And awareness is the primary faculty that can make desires wane and dissolve. From remorse and shame, people devise ways of hurting themselves, and that does not help them eliminate the cause of their suffering. Remorse and shame are found in those who still have self-importance."

I then asked with some hesitation, "Do you mean that desires can be satisfied as long as one is aware?"

Siddhattha said, "Your mind jumps ahead in order to comprehend what is behind, never touching an understanding of what is. For what is present for you right now is the remorse that comes from having committed an action that you feel is not good and wholesome. You have not begun to see the role of desire in all of this. Instead, you perceive yourself as the kind of a person who did a certain deed and wants to do it again, even though you know you will regret it afterward.

"So," he continued, "the desire for sensual pleasures is so strong in you that you can only conceive of ways to satisfy it, and you would use awareness as a means to that end."

His observation of my motives and character, being accurate, stung me deeply. I felt hatred for Siddhattha and then hatred for myself. To save face, I thought that I must surely kill myself. Or, I must get Siddhattha to restore my dignity. Then I would not need to dwell on the hurt that made a home in my heart. But Siddhattha's way was to go through the many rooms of hurt until one discovers the door to nibbana.

With that realization, my mind lightened.

Later that day, I added some new verses to my poem:

In the world, what is the origin of holding things dear
And the longings that get stirred up?
And what is the origin of the hope and the purpose of life
That people hold for their future?

A relentless hunger to be is the origin of holding things dear
And the longings that get stirred up in the world.
This is also the origin of the hope and the purpose
That people hold for their future.

XI

I was curious about what kind of instruction the arahants would give the wandering ascetic. Would they imitate Siddhattha? Or would they teach something of their own making? So I joined the wandering ascetic. I walked with him during the second day of our journey and sat near him when he received instruction from Venerable Sariputta.

Sariputta was slightly younger than Siddhattha, tall and thin, with a handsome face. He had a very pleasant voice and a sharp mind.

He said to the ascetic, "In meditation, know the truth of mind as it is. What is the truth of mind as it is? The mind is wild. It flows where it will. With the inner lord you can stop the flow and tame the mind, and without the inner lord you can do the same. Do you know the difference between the two?"

The ascetic replied, "The inner lord is like an elephant trainer who whips the beast into submission and then gives it a treat when it acts according to command. The mind without the inner lord is like an elephant trainer who speaks gently to the beast, gaining its trust and affection. In time, the elephant learns what is right action and what is not."

At that moment, I decided to insert myself in their conversation because I had never heard the Buddha talk about the inner lord.

"Venerable Sariputta, what is the inner lord?"

He looked at me thoughtfully. Then he said, "Just as Brahma believes that the world is His creation and a manifestation of His Being, so does the inner lord believe that all thoughts, feelings, intentions, and movements are his creation and a manifestation of his being. Like Brahma, the inner lord does not see things as they are, and thus does not know that he too is a creation and is subject to the same conditions as his thoughts, feelings, intentions, and movements. That is, he too will experience the unwelcome changes of loss, death, and rebirth."

I promptly asked Sariputta another question.

"Does everyone have an inner lord?"

Sariputta replied, "No. Arahants are no longer bound by the dictates of an inner lord. We know a deep and profound inner peace free from the delusion of possessing a higher self. The inner lord is starved of nourishment and so perishes."

The ascetic then said, "The elephant is not only trained with gentleness but is wise and gentle to all beings. Such an elephant I have not met. But such people do exist, such as yourself, Venerable Sariputta. I pay homage to this wondrous teaching which uproots all aggression, delusion, and greed."

Sariputta smiled and simply said, "You understand."

They bowed to each other and then parted company.

The night sky was clear and there was a crescent moon. The stars were just coming out as I climbed the small hill above our camp. I wanted to be alone to contemplate Sariputta's teaching. The idea that the mind and the inner lord could be separated was startling to me. My mind and my higher self seemed to be one and the same. I felt a profound mental strain when I tried to isolate the inner lord. It could not be done. If I could not experience the inner lord as distinct from my consciousness, how could I apply what Sariputta had taught to the wandering ascetic?

I closed my eyes and brought my attention to the front of my face. As before when I meditated, I immediately thought about one thing after another. Like Sariputta said: "The mind is wild. It flows where it will." And my mind flowed into thoughts about my future. I made plans for my return home. It felt urgent to tell my father that I was seeking a bride. I wanted to be with a woman. Lust arose. I sat with awareness of how it wrapped around my chest and tickled my lungs, while a definite excitement flowed through my throat and nostrils. The smell of the local shrubs greeted me, and I experienced a distinct awareness of one breath leaving and then another one coming in. This distinct awareness was a manifestation of the inner lord. I could sense a higher intelligence within me and a more powerful concentration than I had ever known. I felt expansive and open to the universe. The gods were nearby. I crossed over into another realm, one where only sages go. Still, when I reflected on what was happening, I could see no separation of my mind from the inner lord. Both were one and the same. Then I remembered Sariputta's words: "Free from the delusion of possessing a higher self, the inner lord is starved of nourishment and so perishes."

I simply did not believe that the higher self, or even my worldly self, was a delusion. Self was the most real thing to me. That was why I experienced the inner lord and my mind as being the same thing. Then what Sariputta taught was not my reality. Once again, I felt doubt arise, filling me with skepticism and distrust.

I heard the sound of bhikkhus chanting in the valley below. Their words professed their faith in the Buddha's teaching. I thought about how they must know something I did not, for all I had was my doubt. I felt the urge to go down into the valley and seek out Siddhattha, for I wanted him to explain Venerable Sariputta's teaching and put my doubt to rest.

As I approached the camp, I heard a horse galloping toward me. I turned to look in its direction, and the rider shouted at me to move out of the way. I jumped aside as horse turned abruptly, stopping a few paces from me. I recognized the horseman. It was Drona.

He said, "I am here on official business. Go tell Siddhattha that King Bimbisara does not trust King Chetaka. He has heard through his spies that King Chetaka is angry that his son has become a bhikkhu. King Bimbisara fears that there is a plot to harm Siddhattha and his followers. It is well known that King Chetaka follows the teachings of Nataputta and would never consider a sage such as Siddhattha, with his huge following and wealthy supporters, to be anything other than a charlatan."

"That is nonsense!" I said. "You are making up a story to cover for your gaming or being with your woman."

Drona yelled, "Foolish boy! It is the truth. Ask Siddhattha. He knows well the leanings of King Chetaka."

Then, as abruptly as he appeared, he vanished. He had no intention of ever being my attendant. Then it dawned on me that Drona occupied a position of authority, trusted by King Bimbisara to carry this important message. And I, being my king's servant, was now Drona's messenger.

XII

Thirty years later, during King Ajatasattu's reign

I am here in Rajagaha at my father's house. My younger brother and his wife live in this house with their five children. My mother passed away seven years ago, but that was not the first time I lost a loved one. My wife died in this very same house giving birth twenty-five years ago. My son did not survive. Since then, I have been here three times on account of the deep sadness that springs from my memory of her.

My father has kept to his bed for the past two days. At first, he was weak in the limbs. Now he sleeps much of the time. My brother told me that when my father wakes up, he usually seems confused, desperately scanning the room, looking for someone who is not there. When someone visits him, he does not recognize who it is. He cannot speak, but once my brother heard him mumbling in his sleep. The physician believes that his soul has been captured by a demon, and that in the darkness of sleep, my father is fighting with the demon over the destiny of his soul.

I sit by my father's side, holding his hand as I listen to his shallow breathing. I have been waiting for him to recognize me and acknowledge that I am attending on him in his final days. I am here out of duty, not love. I am more attached to the appearance of doing what is right than I am to the feelings I have for those close to me.

This is who I am and I cannot change that about me. I lost the one I loved twenty-five years ago. Only then did I understand what Siddhattha meant by holding on to that which is dear as the source of sorrow. I vowed never again to become attached to anyone. So, over the past twenty-five years, I have devoted myself to memorizing the words of ministers, generals, and poets. With my untiring dedication to work, I have been able to periodically banish the anguish of her death from my mind.

I now see that not only I have been living the truth of anguish, I have become its prisoner. I yearn for a way to escape the pain of my own mind, but I have no idea where to begin. If only I had listened with different ears to the words of the arahants three decades ago and applied myself with greater diligence to the noble path they taught, then maybe I would not be in this unfortunate position.

As I sit near my father, I turn my ear to his shallow breathing. His exhalations draw me into myself. I become calm. My inner darkness lifts, though my chest feels like it is being crushed by a boulder. My breathing becomes forced and labored. An impulse to cry rises to my face, but it is a dry cry. My sobs are strangled. I know this grief only too well. I have lost my wife, a life dearer to me than my own. My life is empty and useless. I too will grow old and die, leaving nothing. There is no escape from this kind of suffering. Siddhattha, if your mind can hear my thoughts, tell me the way, appear to me with the way to go through this and come out the other side.

Just at that moment, I hear someone banging on the front door and then the sound of heavy footsteps in the other room. A messenger and two guards have come for me.

The messenger says to me, "King Ajatasattu is displeased with you for leaving Nataputta before he ended his vow of silence. He demands you come with us to his pleasure garden and recall to him the saintly wisdom of the niganthas."

I say, "I must stay here with my father. He is on his deathbed."

One of the guards steps forward and says, "We have our orders. You must come now or receive the king's wrath."

"I see."

As I walk out the door, with a guard on each side, I pray that my father may find a better place than this world for his next existence.

XIII

While I am being escorted across the city of Rajagaha, I think about how to satisfy King Ajatasattu's curiosity and shorten the visit. I am worried that my father might die while I am with the king. It was fortunate for me that guards were sent to escort me, for without them I would surely have returned to my father's side.

The pleasure garden is in a remote part of the royal palace grounds. In the days of King Bimbisara, the king would invite all the noblemen and wealthy merchants of his kingdom, along with their wives and families, to his pleasure garden for music, dance, plays, and religious discourses. The garden was green and lush, with special varieties of flowers and trees. There was a lawn of low-cut grass where King Bimbisara would hold outdoor events. It was twice the size of the large assembly hall in the palace. King Bimbisara would sit on a large round cushion as big as an elephant, surrounded by his wives, the loveliest women in the whole of Magadha. The wealth and beauty of those congregated would take my breath away, and it would be as though I had died and was reborn in the realm of the splendorous gods.

Not so today. King Ajatasattu has obviously let the garden fall to ruin. The expansive lawn of King Bimbisara's assemblies is no more, reduced to patches of dirt where nothing grows except the occasional weed. In the middle of what used to be the assembly area, two gentlemen sit in wooden chairs on an old rug.

One of the men is in his late forties. His frame is gaunt but muscular, and his narrow bearded face looks haggard, as if he has not slept in days. He wears a military uniform. The only thing that distinguishes him from an ordinary officer is his regal necklace.

The other man is short and stocky, though not wrinkled nor flabby, especially for his sixty or more years. His head is shaven, and one could easily mistake him for a bhikkhu. The only thing that sets him apart from one of the Buddha's followers is the color of his robe, which is definitely not a shade of brown or orange. Instead, it is sapphire blue. This is the first time I have seen Devadatta up close.

King Ajatasattu invites me to sit down on the rug in front of him and Devadatta. I approach the king and kneel before him, bowing three times. Then, while still on my knees, I turn to Devadatta and bow three times. Devadatta says a short blessing for my future prosperity and health. I am pleasantly surprised that Devadatta acts like a sage.

I sit down on the threadbare rug in front of the two most powerful men in Magadha. The guards are asked to leave. Once they are gone, I notice my anxiety decrease, though I am still apprehensive about what King Ajatasattu might do to me.

King Ajatasattu looks at me intently and says, "I heard you left Nataputta before he completed his vow of silence. How were you then able to carry out your orders?"

"My Gracious King," I say, "one of the nigantha elders gave a most intelligent discourse on the teachings of Nataputta while I was there. I bring you those words, worthy of a king such as yourself, who seeks sainthood in this very life."

"Then tell me, Chronicler, what did this nigantha elder say?"

"He said that restraint from all harmful action, combined with ascetic practices and vows, leads to the cleansing of the soul. When the soul is pure, it is liberated and enjoys eternal peace and freedom. Nataputta knows this because he has realized the liberation of his soul and has thus become the knower of everything at every time and in every place."

Devadatta smiles at my words and says, "Well said, Chronicler. That is truly Nataputta's teaching in summary. Did you delve into the finer points of how the soul arrives at final liberation?"

"Venerable Sage," I say, being careful to stay on Devadatta's good side, "I could not delve as deeply as someone with your level of intelligence and extraordinary spiritual gifts. As an ignorant layman in these matters, I went only as far as to see how Nataputta's doctrine of restraint differs from those who teach the middle way."

My mention of the middle way must have irritated Devadatta, for he interrupts me and begins speaking angrily.

"Nataputta speaks a truth not founded on speculation. He knows that purification comes about through severe self-restraint, deprivation, and the practice of austere vows. He does not teach a middle way that is pleasing to the masses like my cousin Siddhattha does. Siddhattha cheats people into believing that good actions, compassion, and self-knowledge can lead to final liberation. It is a doctrine pleasing to those who believe that liberation of mind can be achieved without abandoning the comforts of the world. While Siddhattha enjoys fine food, expensive robes, and the best doctors and medicine, Nataputta fasts, wears no clothes, and patiently suffers bodily pain. Which of these two teachers is more worthy of veneration?"

"Venerable Devadatta," King Ajatasattu says, "you yourself have your own teaching that partakes of both paths, that of Nataputta and the Buddha. Is your soul not liberated? Are you not the true teacher of the path to nibbana?"

A flash of rage passes across Devadatta's contracted face. He lets out a barely audible groan.

He says, "The purpose of this life of mine is not to liberate my soul, but to fight and destroy the false teachings and their proponents. That is why I have gained the magical powers you know so well. I am the only one who can put an end to the false Buddha. Siddhattha has convinced people he has realized nibbana, and yet he cannot see into the future and does not even know his exact time of death. How can such a man call himself fully liberated?"

King Ajatasattu turns to face Devadatta and says, "I see what your mission is, but what you are? Are you a bodhisattva, a Mara, or an incarnation of a wrathful god? What are you?"

"Great King," Devadatta says, modulating his voice like a magician, "I am the one who not long ago manifested in your lap as a young boy clad in a girdle of snakes. Impressed by my psychic powers, you honored me by inviting me to sit at your side as you took your father's kingdom from him. I became your trusted friend and ally, without whom you would still be a prince yearning for his father's throne. Look at me, I am your trusted friend and ally, Devadatta. I am your trusted friend and ally, Devadatta...."

JASON SIFF ❋ 45

I can see King Ajatasattu's eyes grow glassy and his body become limp. Suddenly, he slumps down in his chair. His chin rests on his chest.

"It is time for His Majesty's nap," Devadatta says. "Chronicler, please go now. You may stay in Rajagaha until Nataputta ends his vow of silence. But then hurry to his side. Remember! Delve into the finer points as to how the soul reaches final liberation."

XIV

Devadatta has granted me the time to be with my father, but now I know I am to be his servant. My new mission is to get the nigantha's path to liberation like a spy who is sent to steal the enemy's plans of attack. At any moment, I can be called away from my father's side, which makes me uneasy as I continue my vigil.

My father will not succumb to death, and yet his condition does not change for the better. I wonder why this is happening to me. All I know is that it makes me reflect on how my father has influenced my life.

I have lived my life as I believed he would have wanted, though I never asked him directly what that was. During the days when I was King Bimbisara's Chronicler and followed the Buddha to Vesali, I had the idea that if I decided to become a bhikkhu, my father would be heartbroken and forever bitter. Where did this idea come from? Was it from having witnessed the repercussions of the Licchavi prince and his cousins becoming bhikkhus? Perhaps I imagined my father would become enraged like King Chetaka.

But it was not just King Chetaka's reaction. It had to do with the mood of the times. The yearning to become a sage was strong in many young men and women. There were those who succumbed to it and those who resisted it. Those who resisted it were a comfort to their parents, while those who succumbed were abominations. Deep down, I did what I did with my life to comfort my parents by not changing course.

That was my single worst mistake! I sat with the greatest teacher of our age, memorizing his words while I made half-hearted attempts to follow his teaching. Then I walked away to take up a life that was ordinary, comfortable, pleasing to my parents.

I had no courage back then. The journey to Vesali was the first time I had left home and seen my own fears. Even now, I cannot seem to get beyond my fears.

XV

Thirty years earlier, during King Bimbisara's reign

After my attendant rode off, I returned to our camp. If it were indeed true that King Bimbisara did not trust King Chetaka, then I was obligated to make that known to Siddhattha.

I found Siddhattha in his hut with two of his bhikkhus, both of whom I had never seen before. I entered quietly with the hope that my anxiety would be apprehended by those present and that they would stop their conversation and ask me to speak. But that did not happen. Even Siddhattha, who was normally acutely aware of the moods of others, listened to the two bhikkhus without even a glance in my direction. After a few moments, it dawned on me that they were talking about standing in judgment over the questionable actions of another bhikkhu. That was something I had never considered possible, since all bhikkhus were supposed to be beyond reproach. So I put my concerns aside and began to listen carefully to one of the bhikkhus. He was a small, meek man who squinted at Siddhattha as he spoke.

"What I say is true. My fellow bhikkhu here can attest to it."

The other man, who was big and bulky, and did not appear to be very bright, nodded his head in agreement. The near-sighted bhikkhu then went on to ask Siddhattha if he should continue to speak of this matter in my presence, since it was business between bhikkhus and did not concern a layperson like myself. Siddhattha briefly considered my presence and then allowed me to stay. Perhaps he thought it would be worthy of memorization.

The bhikkhu said, "We seek your judgment on a bhikkhu who goes by the name of Siha, 'The Lion.' He is loud, proud, and fierce. He went forth into the bhikkhus' life two years ago when you came to our village. Do you remember this man?"

Siddhattha replied, "I do recall him. He looks and acts like a lion. He is a big man who speaks in a fast, fierce manner, ordering the samaneras about and arguing with the elders."

"That is the man! He was troublesome then and has become even worse. Soon after his going forth, he claimed that he was fully liberated. He persuaded some lay supporters in our village to build him a hut. When the hut was built, he asked them to build an assembly hall. When the hall was built, he asked them for a chair the size of a throne. When the chair was placed in the hall, he asked them to spread the word that Siha the Enlightened One would be speaking in this hall daily, and that everyone should come and give him offerings."

What shocking behavior! I was certain that this Siha was a fraud. Siddhattha should give him some horrible punishment. Imprisonment! Or a public whipping! Siddhattha, however, seemed unperturbed by what he had heard. Instead, he asked the bhikkhu to tell him everything.

"For the first several days, laypeople from the surrounding villages came to see Siha. They asked him for all sorts of boons, and he refused none of them. Most of the people asked him for wealth or for a good marriage arrangement for a son or daughter, but one man asked to obtain the wife of another for his bride, while someone else asked that an enemy of his be stricken with illness. These people gave money and jewels to Siha, who accepted them knowing that these riches were given as payment for their requests being fulfilled.

"Word spread that Siha did not have the magical powers he had led people to believe he possessed. Still, he accepted gifts and proclaimed that he was enlightened, which angered many of the villagers. People stopped coming to see him. His hall became empty. His anger grew. The villagers, who now feared and hated Siha, shut their doors and would not give alms to any bhikkhu. The Blessed One's Sangha was shunned, and so all of the bhikkhus in that part of Magadha left to join the virtuous bhikkhus that reside in Rajagaha. It was there that we heard of your journey to Vesali and saw it as our duty to find you and tell you about this tragedy to the Sangha, the Dhamma, and the good name of the Buddha."

The Buddha said, "This is truly a tragedy to the Sangha, but not so to the teaching and the good name of the Buddha. The Dhamma cannot be grasped by such a man. It exists separate from him. The good name of the Buddha cannot be tarnished by the misguided actions of such a man. It too exists separate from him. But to the Sangha, this man's selfish and ignorant deeds bring shame, slander, and disgrace, so it is from the Sangha that he must be expelled. There is no greater punishment a Buddha can give. In all fairness, however, Siha must appear before me to refute these allegations or admit his deeds before my judgment is passed. Please go back to your village and relay this to him. If he does not wish to comply, then ask him to voluntarily surrender his robes and bowl and return to the life of a householder."

This said, the two bhikkhus bowed to the Buddha, accepting their mission. There was a period of silence once they were gone, during which I noticed that the Buddha was thinking. I imagined that he wanted to talk about what just went on. Instead, he asked me what was on my mind, since I had seemed worried when I first walked in.

I said, "I saw my attendant. He was carrying a message from King Bimbisara."

"What did the king say?"

"King Bimbisara said that King Chetaka is not pleased about his son joining the Sangha. He does not trust King Chetaka and thus fears that there is a plot to harm you and your followers."

"Those who love me," the Buddha said, "fear that harm will come to me. Those who hate me wish me dead. Having uprooted and discarded the craving for renewed existence, it is only my body that is subject to pain, disease, old age and death. Nibbana is devoid of suffering.

"Chronicler, do not be anxious on my behalf. Work diligently for your own liberation. That is the teaching of the Buddhas. Now, I must rest."

XVI

We arrived at the southern bank of the Ganges the very next day. We had expected to find a welcoming party from King Chetaka, but all we found was a newly erected hut. I sat in the hut with the Buddha and four of his bhikkhus. While they were meditating, I composed some additional verses to my poem. They went like this:

What is the source of this relentless hunger to be?
From what source do judgments,
Anger, lies, and suspicions arise?
And those things spoken of by the sages?

This relentless hunger to be arises lifted up by the
      experiences of pleasure and pain in the world.
People are put into turmoil over decisive judgments
And the destruction and creation of what they see.
Anger, lies, suspicions, and those things sages speak of
      arise out of pleasure and pain.
One who doubts would learn,
Following the path of higher knowledge,
Having listened to the teachings of the Great Sage.

XVII

Thirty years later, during King Ajatasattu's reign

I am somewhat thankful that a messenger from the royal court has come for me. Being by my father's bed these last four days has been exasperating. His condition has not improved. There have been moments when I have wished for his death as a way to end his struggle with life. I find myself without any tender feelings for this man who once meant so much to me. That, in a way, does not surprise me.

Perhaps I just need to get back to work. For as soon as I leave the house with the messenger, I feel a certain strength return to my chest and limbs, though my mind is flooded with dread. Devadatta has sent for me.

I am being led to the royal palace this time. I have been there several times and know my way around, but the part of the palace I am taken to is new to me. It is not bright and airy like the palace rooms above ground. I am led down a dark hall to a room that was probably used as servants' quarters. The messenger opens the door to the room. I hesitate for a moment, wishing to flee, but I know I must go through with this. Maybe this is the only way I will ever get free of Devadatta.

Devadatta sits in a nice chair. He has a small table with an oil lamp on it and a glass of some sort of beverage. There is no other chair or bed in the room. The only place to sit is on the mat in front of Devadatta. With a grand gesture, he beckons me to enter and take a seat on the floor.

Devadatta says, "Chronicler, do you remember the last time we met, how I had asked you to get some details about Nataputta's path to nibbana? I want you to know what I need to know, for I cannot waste any more time. I would go myself, but I do not want it bandied about that Devadatta seeks instruction from Nataputta. I am too proud for that."

"Tell me then what you need to know," I obediently reply. "I shall do as you wish."

"First of all, Chronicler, let no one mistake me for a fool. I know the teachings of the middle way set forth by Siddhattha as well as any man alive. I should be the heir to my cousin's Sangha of sages, even though he has declined to give any of his bhikkhus that honor. That means his teaching will most likely perish after his death and a new one, with heirs chosen by me, will live on. Only, I have not found full liberation of mind.

"I have tried all of Siddhattha's instructions. I have tried to see the root of craving, but all I see are separate cravings, like the banyan tree with its many hanging roots, and not the root craving. I have seen the Brahma worlds and gained psychic powers, but none of that has led to liberation. I have tried to see emptiness and no self in all aspects of my consciousness, internally and externally. All I see is pride, jealousy, and rage. From all that I have tried, I cannot believe that Siddhattha teaches the true path to nibbana. I do not believe nibbana comes from understanding, for if anyone should be capable of such understanding..."

As he pauses, I wonder why he is telling me these things about himself. I can only surmise that Devadatta wants me to perceive him as a great man, a brilliant and perceptive man, even though I see him as a proud, envious man.

Devadatta says, "Siddhattha teaches that the mind can attain liberation through awareness, discernment, and understanding. He does not believe in fasting, vows, and austere practices. He says he traveled that path as far as it will go. How does he know that for sure? What if he did not see that path to the end? I believe Siddhattha gave up on it before he arrived at final liberation and took up a path that was easier, nobler in his eyes.

"Many years ago, I followed his instructions on developing dispassion by living at a charnel ground. I observed the corpses in their various stages of decomposition during the day and meditated on those images at night. But every morning, I left the stench of the rotting bodies behind as I went to collect my morning alms. I would then sit under a shade tree, enjoying the spicy food given to me by the faithful. After eating, I would lie down with a full stomach, lulled into tranquility. That is the so-called Buddha's teaching, and that is why it does not work."

Devadatta leans forward. I give him my full attention.

"Chronicler, I know you are the right man for this mission. You have spent time with Siddhattha. You know what he teaches. You have the ability to distinguish between the different teachings and extract the elements that make each of them distinct. But I fear that you are fond of Siddhattha and that you secretly harbor a wish to further his purpose and defeat my own.

"Therefore, I have decided that we will make a pact. If you fail to find out what it is that has enabled Nataputta to reach final liberation and omniscience, you will be tortured and put to death. But if you succeed, and I have in my possession Nataputta's path to nibbana, your life will be spared, and you will be allowed complete freedom to do as you please for the rest of your life. What do you say to these terms?"

I am too scared to speak. I nod my head in assent, bow to Devadatta once, and then raise my head, pleading for compassion with my eyes.

"Chronicler! Do not worry so! Your success is far more likely than your failure. Now leave me! Nataputta broke his vow of silence at the light of dawn. Hurry! Honor our pact. If you decide to flee, your family will suffer in your place."

XVIII

From the royal palace, I go straight to my father's house. I am scared. I need to tell someone about my predicament. Danger is not supposed to get this close. My life as a chronicler for the king has been uneventful and calm for these past thirty years. I have not felt this terrified since the time I accompanied the Buddha to the city of Vesali. But then, it was not my life that was threatened.

I arrive at my father's house to find a guard standing at the door. He has orders not to let me in. I shout to my younger brother inside the house and ask him to come outside. The first thing he tells me is that his family is under house arrest until I return from my mission. Then he asks me what this is all about and I tell him. The whole thing sounds preposterous to me as I say it, though I can tell that my brother takes it seriously and is quick with advice as to how to accomplish my mission.

He says, "It may not be possible to ask Nataputta how he became liberated, for he may not have the words to convey it. Instead, observe him and take note of every unusual, saintly thing he does. There is no better way to satisfy Devadatta's curiosity than to give him an elaborate picture of Nataputta's way of life, presenting every detail, as if each one is the key to success."

I thank my brother, for he is wise when it comes to political matters, even though he did not follow in my father's footsteps and become a minister. He held himself back from politics and chose a career in trade, specializing in cloth, linen, and silk. His advice sounds to me like the strategy he used to acquire secret dyeing techniques from his competitors in other provinces, which he did as a young man to increase his business and establish himself as one of the leading merchants of Magadha. My father was very proud of his business acumen. Now, I too feel a surge of pride at my brother's cleverness.

I leave the city and soon find the footpath that leads to where I last saw Nataputta. I walk with my fear in the background, nudging at me but not interfering with my sense of purpose. This mood would have lasted much longer but for the discovery, when I finally arrive after hours of walking in the afternoon heat, that Nataputta left early this morning on a journey. One of the nigantha sages believes that Nataputta is on his way to Vesali to end his life by starvation.

That is not what I want to hear. At first, I am distressed by this news and feel like crying, but then I realize that this can be used to my advantage if I am able to find Nataputta and spend some time observing him closely. Then I will be giving Devadatta an account of Nataputta's last days and what he did to secure his final liberation from rebirth.

I walk in the direction of the road to the Ganges, the same road I had walked thirty years ago with the Buddha. I see an old man, naked, walking slowly not far ahead of me. Disregarding my brother's advice altogether, I decide to walk up to Nataputta and engage him in conversation. That way I might learn a little something that I could bring back to Devadatta.

Nataputta is wearing a piece of cloth covering his mouth and nose. As he walks, he sweeps the ground before him with a small broom. I was told by a nigantha sage that they will do this when they go on a journey. This detail must be mentioned in my report.

I tap Nataputta on the shoulder in a friendly way. He ignores me. Then I try walking ahead and standing in front of him. He slowly makes his way toward me, sweeping the ground. When he notices my feet, he stops and looks up into my eyes.

"Great Sage," I say, "I come from the court of King Ajatasattu to learn Mahavira's path to sainthood."

Nataputta keeps staring at me as though my words are incomprehensible. He looks harder and harder, searching for something within my eyes, and then he speaks to me.

"You were sent by that wicked sage, Devadatta, to uncover how the soul becomes fully liberated. Tell Devadatta that the deepest and darkest hell awaits him when it is his time. He will endure pain that is a thousand times that which he inflicted on others. There is no escape for him from the realms of torment, so how could there be a liberation for him from the happy realm of human birth?"

"Nataputta," I implore, "I will be tortured and killed if I do not bring Devadatta your secret. Please have compassion."

"Devadatta will not kill you, an insignificant man. Instead, he will use you to kill Siddhattha Gotama."

"How is that possible?" I ask, filled with awe.

"I have already told you more than you need to know. Now leave me to my path and get yourself back to yours."

I am ashamed of myself for having assumed that Nataputta was in league with King Ajatasattu and Devadatta. Now, I can see that he is a seer, a true sage who practices what he teaches and gives what teaching he can. Though I may never be inclined to follow Nataputta's austere path, I am grateful for his visionary powers. I only hope he is right about Devadatta not killing me and wrong about me being the instrument of Siddhattha's death.

I decide to walk discreetly behind Nataputta, and, over the next few days, learn what I can about his rituals, his conduct, and his spiritual presence.

XIX

Thirty years earlier, during King Bimbisara's reign

We woke up to the birds squawking at dawn, sleeping as we did on the sandy banks of the Ganges. The bhikkhus held a meeting where they shared their collective concerns about Siddhattha entering Vesali. I joined their meeting in the middle, since I had to wash up and brush my robe to make sure that I would be presentable to the nobles of the Licchavi clan. For some reason, I had forgotten about my attendant's warning, though I soon recalled his words when I listened closely to the concerns being voiced by the bhikkhus.

An elder bhikkhu by the name of Koṇḍañña was speaking. He said, "It is apparent from this message, received from King Chetaka before the light of dawn, that he does not wish to hear the Buddha teach nor let his subjects give shelter and alms to his bhikkhus. Instead, he wants only his son and nephews to join him in his court, and then requests that Siddhattha perform a miracle to prove that he is the Buddha. I cannot see any reason why we should continue on this journey."

The bhikkhus voiced their unanimous agreement with Venerable Koṇḍañña. Siddhattha then spoke with the strength and conviction I had grown fond of hearing.

"The grief of King Chetaka is great, and so all of you believe that his rage and cruelty may be great as well. The Buddha does not refuse to teach anyone on account of fear, so I shall continue on this journey to Vesali. And the miracle the Licchavi King wishes of me is not mine to grant, but he should be told that his wish will come true if the conditions are right."

"What is this miracle?" I wondered aloud. One of the bhikkhus standing nearby whispered in my ear, "Vesali has not had enough rain this past year. 'If Siddhattha is truly the Buddha, then let him bring rain.' That is King Chetaka's request."

Siddhattha said, "Many of you worship me as a god and protect me as though I were a king. I am neither of these. Let the Buddha's wisdom guide the Sangha. Then let us be done with all this talk. For as we speak of fears and concerns that are but conjurations of a powerful magician, the rest of the world lives, and we are dead to its call. To be always awake and alert in the mind, present in the sense doors, and sustained by knowledge and compassion, that is the path to freedom from worry and care."

A young bhikkhu said, "You teach about freedom from worry and care from having overcome fear and craving. For those of us who do not know the complete cessation and non-return of fear and craving, your words give us a little knowledge of the path.

Please, Venerable Siddhattha, give us the whole knowledge of the path that leads to the abandoning of fear."

The Buddha said, "Just as I cannot perform miracles, I cannot give anyone the whole knowledge of the path. That knowledge arises when the conditions are right. There needs to be clouds, wind, and moisture in the air for it to rain. Just so, there needs to be tranquility, clarity, and discerning intelligence in the mind for it to see existence for what it is. It comes from within you and is not dependent on my words or presence. And you are right. I give only a little knowledge, for that is all the knowledge anyone can give to another."

For the first time in all these weeks with the Buddha, I heard him say something that made immediate sense to me. Maybe it was the place, standing on the south bank of the holy river, that granted me the ability to contemplate what Siddhattha said as fully as I could. I knew he was right. I could only find the whole knowledge of the path within me.

A middle-aged bhikkhu said, "If you cannot give knowledge to another, then why do you have so many followers? I left my wife and children because I heard that you knew the path to nibbana within this very lifetime. And now you tell me that you cannot impart that knowledge."

The Buddha said, "A little knowledge is not enough, but it is all that is possible. If I could liberate all the beings in the world, I would. But it is not possible even for a Buddha to give the path of liberation to someone who has not awakened it within himself."

My mind drifted as the Buddha continued to speak. I heard the sound of his words, but not their meaning. No matter what Siddhattha would now say, I felt that I agreed with him. Had I vanquished doubt? I was not about to develop such a conceit. So, I banished that thought from my mind.

XX

Not long after the morning meal, a huge raft carrying several men landed on our side of the shore. Ghosa, the minister to King Chetaka, was their leader. Four other noblemen and ten soldiers accompanied him. It seemed odd to me that soldiers were sent to greet sages, which gave credence to my fear that Siddhattha's life was in danger.

Siddhattha and many of the bhikkhus went to meet the raft. I followed behind them. When they stopped to surround Ghosa and his men, I made my way through the crowd to stand where I could hear everything clearly.

Ghosa said, "Venerable Siddhattha, have you agreed to King Chetaka's request?"

"It will rain in Vesali regardless of my presence. Can you feel the moisture in the air? How the breeze speeds up and then slows down?"

"King Chetaka will be pleased to see you then."

"I have no objection to meeting King Chetaka," Siddhattha said. "But I do object to the king sending his soldiers to greet his son and nephews."

"We will not harm the prince and his cousins. King Chetaka and his ministers believe that if they can just have a moment alone with the young men to outline what they have forfeited by becoming bhikkhus, then they might reconsider. Since they were ordained in haste, the true consequences of their sacrifice may not have been evident to them. Please allow King Chetaka to give his son another chance to claim his worldly inheritance."

Siddhattha said, "It is not for me to allow or restrain the former prince. The choice is his. The Buddha does not bind people to him. But can we say the same of your mighty king?"

"Very well," Ghosa said, ignoring Siddhattha's last comment, "we will take the prince and his cousins with us and then send the raft back for you and your bhikkhus."

"But first, Minister Ghosa," Siddhattha said, "you must ask them if they approve of your plan. It is their choice to reconsider their going forth as bhikkhus. If they do not wish to return to the lay life, then please allow them to remain here with their brothers and enter Vesali in their company."

Ghosa's face reddened and bulged at this suggestion. Yet his voice was well-controlled.

"I cannot allow the Licchavi Crown Prince to choose not to see his father. That would go against King Chetaka's will. His rage is fierce, and I should fear for my life if I fail to bring his son back to the palace."

Siddhattha said, "Then, it is you who cannot choose his life course for himself, even though you have wealth and status in the world. The former prince saw this truth and so decided to take appropriate action. And you, who can see it now, remain convinced that you can do nothing to change your situation. Why would you, an intelligent well-meaning man, want these young men to accept an existence as restricted and fearful as your own?"

Ghosa stood still for a minute. It was as though Siddhattha was holding out some bait on a string and drawing Ghosa closer to the Dhamma as he spoke.

"Venerable Siddhattha," Ghosa said, "your logic has caught me in its net. I have always been a good servant to my king and have thought only of our country's welfare. And yet here I am, thinking of my own welfare and that of the former prince. I will listen to your words and if I see the merit in your way, I will renounce my station in life and join your Sangha."

"Then, I will tell you how a bhikkhu lives," Siddhattha said. "He eats once a day, taking food in moderation and not storing any of it for another day. Each day he walks into town with his alms bowl in both hands, his head bent down. He goes from one house to another, accepting alms from one household that day. He takes his alms to a secluded place, eating his food mindfully, knowing the taste of each morsel. He spends his time in meditation and in intelligent conversation, learning from his own observations and those of others. When he meditates, he does no harm to his body. Instead, he cultivates a relaxed body and a flexible mind conducive to introspection. When he speaks, he utters truthful words, friendly words, wise words. He does not speak ill of others and does not cause one person to hate another through his speech. When he engages in contemplation, he goes over in his mind the fruitful knowledge he has heard, bringing his own understanding to the wise words of the Buddha. His time is his own."

"I see what he does," Ghosa said, "but what does he become?"

Siddhattha said, "He becomes free of any further becoming. Let no one assume that a soul attains liberation. It is liberation purified of self-becoming: Nibbana."

"Are you sure that nibbana can be attained in one lifetime, Siddhattha?"

"Yes, I say to you, Ghosa, nibbana awaits you in this life."

"Then, from this day forth, I renounce my position as minister to King Chetaka and take the vows of a bhikkhu."

"Then, from now on," Siddhattha said, "You will be known as Ghosananda."

Soon after giving Minister Ghosa his new name, Siddhattha instructed two bhikkhus to help prepare him for ordination.

XXI

Siddhattha invited the four noblemen who accompanied Minister Ghosa to stay for Ghosananda's ordination. They initially accepted, but after a while one of them asked Siddhattha what they should until then.

Siddhattha replied, "Rest, relax, enjoy the surroundings and the company of bhikkhus. We will make our way across the river to the city of Vesali at another time."

Then a second nobleman, who appeared agitated by the day's events, addressed Siddhattha, "What if King Chetaka is alarmed by our delay? Should we send a messenger to tell him why we are late? And, what shall we now do that Ghosa has become a bhikkhu?"

"Do as you see fit," Siddhattha said.

The four noblemen talked amongst themselves and then boarded the raft with their soldiers, leaving us without a raft to cross the Ganges. I wanted to yell to them to come back and take me with them. I was growing anxious about seeing Vesali. I was certain that my future bride was waiting for me there. I feared that if I did not enter Vesali soon, her and I would never meet. I became sad and withdrew to the little hut where I stayed the night before.

As I napped, new verses to my poem appeared to me in Siddhattha's voice. This happened as my consciousness moved between sleep and waking. When I woke up, I immediately added these two stanzas:

What is the source of pleasure and pain?
In the absence of what do these not become?
Tell me, from what source is creation and destruction?

The source of pleasure and pain involves the senses making
contact with their objects.
In the absence of sense contact, pleasure and pain do not arise.
I tell you that it is from the mind touching the world that
creation and destruction arise.

XXII

I passed much of the remainder of the day by the river. Birds flew above the water hunting for fish. I remember seeing a bird with a fish flapping in its beak as it soared high into the air to seek out a place to eat its prey. I did not recognize this as violence, but as nature, the way of animals. As I reflected on what I saw, I recollected the Buddha's words on how the animal realm is completely dominated by the emotion of fear and is not as happy as the human realm. This recollection led me to contemplate how the human realm is so full of danger that I would not swiftly conclude that it is a happy realm. The Buddha once said that it is due to the precariousness of human life that we can develop in wisdom far more than the gods who truly live in a happy realm. Somehow, I would rather believe that in a truly happy realm, one would have little to upset one's pursuit of knowledge. But back then, I still did not understand what the Buddha meant by wisdom.

I felt like I was wasting the whole afternoon sitting by the river. Siddhattha was not talking to anyone, having decided to spend the rest of the day in meditation. The other bhikkhus were either meditating or in small groups engaged in discussion. Ghosananda was receiving instruction from one of the elder bhikkhus, while the young prince and his cousins were among those who sat in meditation.

For the first time in all those weeks around Siddhattha and his bhikkhus, I felt that I did not really belong in their community. My interests were so different. I would rather have been memorizing someone's words. At that particular moment, however, I would have rather been in Vesali, where I could be asking the Licchavi noblemen about their unmarried daughters and nieces.

That evening I slept fitfully and woke before dawn. The morning mist rose above the plain and turned into fog over the river. Someone shouted that a raft was approaching our shore. Then someone else corrected that report, announcing that three large rafts were approaching.

The first raft carried several noblemen and their footmen. The second carried King Chetaka, his queen, along with her handmaidens, and about twenty soldiers. The third was empty except for the boatman.

Siddhattha sat on a huge rock by the river. Several bhikkhus joined him there to wait for King Chetaka's entourage. I quickly dressed and washed, reaching the riverbank just as King Chetaka and Siddhattha were exchanging greetings.

King Chetaka was a heavy-set man, a giant of sorts, with a thick long beard and hairy arms.

Siddhattha addressed King Chetaka first.

"I am honored by your visit, Great King."

King Chetaka said, "I have come to debate certain points of your doctrine. I would like my son and his cousins to listen closely to what I say, for I hope to persuade them to abandon this way of life."

I was awed by King Chetaka's pride and confidence. If this were to be a test of resolve and not wisdom, then he would surely win this debate with Siddhattha.

Siddhattha asked, "What points would you care to debate? I am ready to address whatever questions you have about the path that leads to the end of sorrow and greed."

"That is precisely what I wish to discuss with you. People say that you profess a law of how things come to be. What do you call this doctrine?"

Siddhattha said, "I call it the law of dependent co-arising. When there is consciousness, there must also be a body and a mind. And, in the same way, dependent on a body and a mind, the six sense realms come to be."

King Chetaka said, "In this teaching of one thing arising dependent on another, it is said that suffering arises from the presence of craving. But it has been my understanding, and that of several sages in my kingdom, that craving arises on account of suffering and not the other way around."

This argument made perfect sense to me. Suddenly, I felt as though I had been tricked by Siddhattha.

King Chetaka continued, "When my son left to join your Sangha, I experienced extreme anguish, from which my desire to have him back grew. That desire consumed me and made me think of abducting my son and inflicting pain on you, his teacher. My body burned, my limbs ached, and my chest felt as though stabbed by a knife. I could not sleep, and no form of pleasure offered by my wives was able to comfort me. Thus, my desire to get my son back was fueled by anguish. I know no other way to extinguish that anguish except to have my son back."

Sympathy for King Chetaka welled up within me, as did hatred for Siddhattha. At that moment, I knew I could never do to my father what the young prince had done to his.

Siddhattha said, "King Chetaka, I can see how you arrived at this view of suffering as the source of desire and not the other way around. In the world of appearances, all types of illusions are created, and our experiences follow the course the illusions create. These illusions do not lead us to the truth. Your desire for your son existed before your son was born and has remained in you ever since. It has been fed by the pleasure you have taken in him and your ambitions for his life. From that desire, you have made him into an image that you love and cherish. That is why you cling to him. The image you have of him is not him, but your own grasping and clinging. And it is because of clinging that you experience anguish over his loss and plot to abduct him. The original desire comes from the delusion that your son is your possession, while the compounded desire arises out of the suffering brought on by your son acting as his own master."

King Chetaka was thunderstruck by Siddhattha's argument. He stood there like a rock until one of his ministers approached him and said something in his right ear. He trembled, looked around, stammered a few syllables, and then faced Siddhattha.

He said, "How did you twist what I said to suit your own purpose? Surely, you possess a power over the thoughts of others. By this magic did you win over my son and nephews?"

Siddhattha replied, "Ask them yourself. I deceive no one when I lay open what is there for everyone to see."

Siddhattha motioned everybody to leave. He apparently wanted King Chetaka to speak with his son and nephews in private. I wanted to see what would transpire, so I crouched down behind a bush.

XXIII

From my hiding place, I watched King Chetaka look up into the sky. He stared at the billowy clouds forming over the city of Vesali to the north. As his attention drew inward, his eyes became glassy, reflecting back a speck of white formed in the blackness of his eyeballs. Then he laughed. I could see his whole body shake with laughter. He turned around to see if anyone was watching, and then raised his head to the sky again. He roared with laughter. Then he settled down, rapidly drawn inward.

King Chetaka's son walked toward his father with his three cousins following behind. They were cleanly shaven, wearing newly washed robes, radiating light that was as much their own as it was the sun's. They did not bow to King Chetaka but appeared to wait for him to bow to them. The king stood there, not showing the proper respect for bhikkhus, so they sat on the ground and motioned to King Chetaka to sit opposite them. He declined with a hand gesture and began to pace in front of them.

King Chetaka said, "By our choices our lives are made, not solely by our birth. You did not know the choices open to you, my son. Instead, you assumed that you could only be a king. And that frightened you. Is that why you have chosen this life as a sage?"

The prince, who now went by the name of Sukha, answered his father, speaking in a firm voice.

"My choice was not made on account of fear, nor was it made because I was unaware of other choices. You may find it hard to comprehend, but my choosing this way of life had nothing to do with you, our people, or the world. It had to do with an anguish in my heart. Only Siddhattha and his arahants know how to lift that anguish. With it gone, I have no need to choose any other way of life."

The king stood perplexed by what he heard. I could see his mouth move, as if to ask a question or to insert his disbelief, but no words emerged.

Then, with added vigor, and a trace of sorrow, King Chetaka said, "You speak of the end of your own anguish, but what of your mother's anguish, my anguish, the anguish of our friends, our people, our allies? You have destroyed all possibility of a happy future. It is as though you have killed yourself!"

Sukha jumped to his feet and began speaking to his father in a direct, disrespectful manner.

"I have destroyed all ambition within me, and so cannot have the future you want for me. I have not killed myself but have killed my passion and greed. I have ended hate and so have no inner conflict about anything I have done. The present is filled with peace and joy, and the future holds contentment and happiness. Can you not see that you are the root of your anguish?"

"No, I cannot! You have caused this anguish!" King Chetaka said. I heard such agony in his voice that I shed a tear.

"I believe you can," Sukha said. "Your eyes are blind because you seek to see what you wish was here instead."

"And what is it that I wish to see?"

"You wish these mendicant robes were royal robes. That this shaven head was full of hair, and that you could place your regal crown upon it on your deathbed. That this clearing was a parade ground and that you were honoring me for my bravery in battle instead of trying to coax me away from my chosen way of life. Your wishes are fanciful, though they appear real. They lead to future miseries and deaths, though you believe in your heart they must lead to joy and happiness. You can only see what you want to see and cannot see what is always here to be seen."

"And what is that? What is it that is always here to be seen?"

Sukha took a deep breath and fixed his gaze on his father. They stared into each other's eyes for a few moments. I could see King Chetaka's muscles begin to relax, and soon after that, he seemed to grin.

Sukha backed away and said, "The human body is what it is and nothing more. It is made up of skin and hair, flesh and meat, bones and nerves, internal organs and fluids. Our feelings are just what they are. We feel pain and pleasure in the world of the senses, just as we can also experience existential pain and meditative bliss. These feelings are not special. They do not make us exalted or inferior. They merely tell us what we feel. Our thoughts are just what they are. We think about what we want, what we hate, and what makes us feel good or bad, and these are all just thoughts upon which the ignorant base their actions. Wise men know that ignorance can be destroyed by uprooting the imagination of self-existence. With your eyes covered in dust, there is only your world, and that world is filled with anguish. Clean the dust from your eyes! See that the world is not yours, but is... is... is."

A new light shone from King Chetaka's eyes. It was not the white speck of reflected light from the clouds that I had seen earlier, nor was it formed in blackness. It was as though a cover had been lifted from his mind. The wisdom that was there could now shine through.

I believed I had witnessed the Buddha's cure. I thought I knew what it looked like from the outside. But, then, I also knew that I did not know what it looked like from inside my own mind.

XXIV

The rest of the morning was uneventful. The bhikkhus ate their meal silently, served by the queen and her maidservants. After eating, many of the bhikkhus found a spot in the shade to sit and meditate. I too sat in the shade, musing.

I worried about whether I was ever going to visit Vesali. Everything seemed so precarious. I had witnessed strong-willed men have their world views changed, and that made it seem as though all was in flux and in danger of being altered. The Buddha seemed to possess the power to change people's way of seeing things, and no one who had contact with him was immune.

He said that he no longer created kamma. All around me was evidence that he did. This puzzled me. He was a world-changer who did not create the kamma that leads to rebirth. I thought about this for a few minutes and concluded that it was a paradox, for all actions that produce change also produce repercussions on account of change, and the most inevitable result of change is the death of something old and the birth of something new.

What I had seen in King Chetaka's eyes seemed to live for just that moment. He did not renounce the world as did his minister, Ghosa. On the other hand, he gave up trying to coax his son back into the world.

My musings were cut short by a messenger announcing that anyone who wished to cross the Ganges and enter Vesali should board the raft.

I ran to get my sack of clothes. When I got to the raft, there were already a dozen bhikkhus on it. I was the last person to board. The Buddha, apparently, intended to stay behind.

My time with the Buddha and his bhikkhus was fairly quiet. Even the suspicion of a plot on the Buddha's life did not disrupt the calm monotony that let time slip by. Surrendering to their way of life, my mind began to slowly blossom from within, tucked away from involvement in the world of kings, commerce, and women. This was going on within me in such a gentle, unassuming way, feeling to me as a natural part of myself, that when I entered Vesali and saw the crowded streets and heard the urban sounds, I instantly became consumed by something so intoxicating that I completely forgot who I was. I saw myself as a handsome nobleman, given a regal entrance to the great metropolis of our age. I imagined myself to be the envy of all the noblemen and the beloved of all the young, eligible women of noble birth.

My perception of myself changed upon some new sense contact, as I then understood it, which made me a different man than I was but a moment before. If this is what the Buddha had meant by no self, then I realized that truth at that very moment. But as I think about it now, in retrospect, I did not know anything for sure, especially such a profound truth.

What happened the rest of the day I cannot recall. I must have fallen asleep as we neared Chetaka's palace. I woke up in a soft and magnificent bed in a large guest room somewhere in the royal palace. Guards stood at my door, not on the outside as would be customary for a guest, but inside the room with me. This startled me. I felt confused again as to who or what I was and how I ought to be treated, wondering if I should be flattered or outraged.

I chose to be level-headed. I asked the guards a few questions regarding where I was, how I had gotten there, and what the plans for me were. I gradually ascertained that King Chetaka was hosting a grand supper, originally planned to celebrate his son's return as the crown prince. The guards did not know that the prince would not be returning with his father, and I was not about to tell them.

The banquet hall was able to hold over a hundred people. We sat at long wooden tables. I was seated far from King Chetaka, where I enjoyed the company of some Licchavi noblemen, speaking to them of my future plans, letting them know that my time for marriage had arrived and I was seeking a bride. I created some interest in a few of my listeners, who invited me to visit them during my stay. This pleased me greatly and made me feel confident that the journey to Vesali would end with me finding a wife after all.

After the meal, people rose from their seats and many of them went for a stroll in the garden, which was illuminated by lanterns. It was fragrant with the scent of night-blooming flowers. There were many narrow paths that led in all directions, some of them uphill, others to caves or sunken ponds.

It was cooler in Vesali, the air had more moisture, so the plants were greener and heartier. Such a contrast to the dry heat of Rajagaha! It was hard for me to imagine returning home. Then it became hard for me to believe that any woman in her right mind would leave this paradise behind. The thought occurred to me that I might have to break with custom and live in my wife's ancestral home instead of my own.

In another part of the garden, I saw King Chetaka surrounded by guards, talking with some noblemen as they admired a large flowering bush. It was hard for me to equate this man, who was acting with such ease and familiarity, with the distraught man I had seen earlier that day.

He noticed me from a distance and motioned me to approach. I walked toward him confidently, pulling my back upright and puffing out my chest. When I was within a few feet of the king, the people around him parted. I stopped in front of him and bowed.

King Chetaka said, "Welcome, Chronicler."

"I am honored to be in your presence," I said.

"Let me ask you this: How does Siddhattha win over his disciples? Is it by clever words? By magical powers? Tell me, how does he do it?"

"I have asked myself that same question. He is genuinely honest. He is not moved by greed, but by compassion. Perhaps it is his compassion that wins everyone over."

"You say honest. That is a good word for it. He is so honest that everyone has to believe him. That is how he won over my son."

"Your majesty, I was present at your son's first meeting with Siddhattha, and later on, I was a witness at his ordination...."

King Chetaka gave me such a look of disdain that I stopped talking. He obviously was unaware that he scowled at me, for he wondered aloud why I had become quiet all of a sudden, and then he pressed me to go on.

I said, "Siddhattha once remarked that your son was won over before they had even met. He said that your son had found within himself the very same teaching Siddhattha discovered as an ascetic. Siddhattha merely added his wisdom to that already acquired by your son."

King Chetaka looked astonished.

"You mean to say that a prince who lived a sheltered life and never had to want for anything was able to discover, unaided, a spiritual teaching known only by sages? That is impossible to believe!"

"Nonetheless, it is so!" I said, for a moment forgetting that I was disagreeing with a powerful king.

"Young Nobleman," King Chetaka said, "you must know that I am the uncle of the renowned nigantha, Nataputta, and am a firm believer in the true liberation of heart realized by the nigantha sages. What you are saying is that anyone here, at any time, can become fully liberated. That does not make sense."

"I do not know the teaching of the nigantha, Nataputta," I said. "But, I know that the path Siddhattha teaches is not that simple."

"If it is not that simple, then enlighten me as to its difficulty."

I took a deep breath and then attempted my first public explanation of the Dhamma.

I said, "Venerable Siddhattha teaches a way that goes between the extremes, never touching them. Within all extremes are the creation of oppositions, and oppositions create conflict. A sage starves himself because he is opposed to eating well and enjoying food. He thinks that he is doing it for liberation when he is really doing it in reaction to what he believes does not lead to liberation. The path to liberation is not in taking vows or not taking them, but in going between the extremes."

King Chetaka motioned me to stop speaking.

He yawned and said, "I am sorry, young man, but I cannot follow what you are telling me. It has been a long day and my mind has been strained. Please stay with us. Enjoy what my palace has to offer."

I bowed humbly and walked away in search of a quiet place where I could be alone with my thoughts. The most nagging thought of all was that I was wrong about what true understanding looked like from the outside. Can someone have an eye-opening experience, perhaps understanding one part of the Dhamma, and then be ignorant of the other parts? Is that how people gradually come to understand the Buddha's path to nibbana?

The thought that the Dhamma is understood in parts over a span of time gave me more to think about as I sat on a bench under the night sky. I listened to the crickets, savored the fragrant, cool breeze, and let my mind return to the realm of the sages. It felt good, at that moment, to have no earthly cares or ambitions.

XXV

Thirty years later, during King Ajatasattu's reign

Over the last two days, I have been shadowing Nataputta, observing him closely whenever I can. I have not discovered anything I do not already know about the nigantha's practices of purification. That is, until now.

I watch from a short distance as Nataputta approaches a small village. He is suddenly surrounded by several boys. They taunt him. They throw stones at him. They yell out offensive names. They stand in his way, forcing him to walk around their village.

Nataputta completely ignores the taunts, the abuse, and the rocks the boys throw at him, apparently unshaken by this kind of attack. He keeps walking with his head down, sweeping the ground in front of him as he goes. He does not quicken his pace nor avert his attention. It is as though the mean actions of the village boys do not exist in Nataputta's world.

I decide to linger in this small village and ask the villagers some questions as to why they let their children throw stones at

a revered sage. An elderly gentleman who witnessed the whole
event, yet did nothing to stop it, simply tells me that they do not
like naked ascetics entering their village. He goes on to say that
they believe that their children should not be exposed to the
ugliness of poverty and starvation, and that the nakedness of the
niganthas is shameful and not worthy of respect. I ask him where
he heard these ideas and he tells me that a bhikkhu who lives
nearby gives discourses on honoring bhikkhus and bhikkhunis
with offerings; and, in the same discourse, this bhikkhu tells
them to curse the nigantha sages and chase them away.

This is not the first time I have heard about a bhikkhu speaking his own narrow-minded views in the name of the Buddha.
An intense hatred for that bhikkhu rises within me. Along with
it comes the desire to tell these poor, ignorant villagers what the
Buddha truly teaches on such matters. I ask the old villager to
announce that King Bimbisara's Chronicler would like to give a
discourse on the Buddha's teaching of non-harming.

I am suddenly surrounded by the men and women of the
village. The very same children who were so cruel to Nataputta
now stand passively next to their parents.

"I have spent a great amount of time memorizing the words
of Siddhattha Gotama, the Buddha of this age. Listen to me well,
for I do not speak my own views but those of the fully awakened
Buddha. What you have heard from a certain bhikkhu is not the
true teaching of the Great Sage, for Siddhattha denounces the
intentional harming of other beings. He denounces the planting,
watering, and nurturing of hate. He does not judge an individual's
character by the views and practices he holds dear.

"Be friendly to everyone you meet. Create that kamma which
brings lasting happiness to all. Welcome sages of all persuasions,
honor them for their individual merit, and show compassion and
understanding for their flaws."

After speaking to the villagers, I turn to see how far Nataputta
has walked. Not far from the village, I see a small cloud of dust
shrouding the hunched-over ascetic, churned up by his constant
sweeping. I walk toward the moving cloud of dust, marveling at
how well I can speak when roused to do so.

I catch up with Nataputta in a matter of minutes. No doubt I step on an insect or two, but that does not concern me. Nataputta stops and turns to face me. I can see in his eyes that he wants to tell me something. I sense that this is it, the end of my assignment.

Nataputta's voice is raspy. I wonder when he last had a sip of water.

"My followers save lives by not killing. Siddhattha's followers will instigate wars. They will fight over subtle and trivial points of doctrine. They will be kings and generals who inflict cruelty and slavery on their people. Wars will be fought because Siddhattha lived and taught. No wars will follow upon my teaching, and my followers will not argue with each other over the doctrine. The path I teach through my example harms no being, great or small, and sets every nigantha free."

I open my mouth to speak, but Nataputta's eyes, which are so clear and bright for an old man, silence me.

"I will be misunderstood," he says, "because future followers of the Buddha will corrupt Siddhattha's teaching, just as you have witnessed. It is a universal law in the human realm that one teacher's followers destroy the teachings of another. That is how ignorance is kept alive. It thrives on the destruction of good and wise teachings.

"Chronicler, listen, remember my words. Let it be known that I live this teaching: It is better to live not wanting anything from the world. That is true liberation of mind! I will die without shame, without regret, and so shall Siddhattha. We traveled different paths yet arrived at the same destination. My life, not my words, reveals that truth."

Nataputta then turns his attention to sweeping his next step clean of all visible life. How many tiny creatures will I kill, unintentionally, on my journey back to Rajagaha? Unaware of stepping on them, I will not be able to count.

XXVI

Thirty years earlier, during King Bimbisara's reign

I spent a week in Vesali. The Buddha's prediction of rain turned out to be true, which greatly impressed King Chetaka and his subjects. This created more interest in me, as I became known as Siddhattha's Chronicler, even though I corrected everyone with the fact that I was still, and will always be, King Bimbisara's Chronicler. Needless to say, people gathered around me to hear my stories of living with the Buddha and his bhikkhus, though I was careful to never again mention that I had witnessed their crown prince's ordination. Along the way, I captured the hearts of a few women, but only one was able to capture mine.

Telling it this way makes it sound as though I acted with confidence and ease. Yes, I was bold about stating my intention of finding a bride, but when it came to someone I admired, I was shy in her presence. She was far too attractive for someone like me, but she liked how I remembered everything she said.

Her father desired a military man for a son-in-law. At the time, I was afraid her father would demand that I prove myself in combat to win her hand. Fortunately, he was satisfied by the fact I was distantly related to King Bimbisara and that my father was a minister to the Great King. I was overjoyed when he agreed to let me marry his daughter.

My destiny was now sealed in such a way that I was not going to become a bhikkhu. My father would be proud. Not only had I made a good choice in marriage, but I also chose a life in accordance with my family's station in the world.

On my last day in Vesali, instead of composing a parting verse for my beloved, I reflected on some of Siddhattha's words and put them into verse:

What is the source of contact in the world?
And how do possessions come to be?
In the absence of what does selfishness not arise?
In the extinguishing of what do our senses stop making contact?

Sense contact arises depending on the presence of a body
    and a mind.
Possessions have their source in the wishing for them.
When there is no wishing for anything,
There is no selfishness.
In the extinguishing of sensation, perception, and ideation,
The mind stops touching the world.

XXVII

As I left King Chetaka's palace, the dark clouds began to part and liberate the blue sky. The road was muddy and there were puddles every few steps, but that did not bother my horse. Everyone I passed recognized the horse as coming from King Chetaka's stables. They looked up at me and clasped their hands in respect. I acknowledged their displays of respect by bowing my head to each of them as I slowly ambled toward the city gates and beyond.

When I was in Vesali, no one told me what had happened to the Buddha. As far as I knew, he never entered the city. As I looked across the Ganges to where we had camped just a week before, I was overcome with a strong desire to see Siddhattha one last time.

The raft came to my side of the shore. The boatman and I sat on the riverbank as he waited for other passengers.

"Tell me, do you know where Siddhattha has gone?"

The boatman said, "The Buddha and his bhikkhus left a couple of days ago."

"Which direction did they go?"

"They went north. I heard a rumor that a wealthy merchant is building a monastery for the Buddha in Savatthi."

"Savatthi? How far is that?"

"It is a good five-day journey on horseback."

"Which road is it?"

He lifted his arm and pointed at a trail leading through the plains to the northwest. I took out my purse and gave him a kahapana for this information. Then I rode off in that direction.

Riding by myself, I was utterly alone. I cried often that day. I was angry at myself for leaving Siddhattha's side to fulfill my own selfish ambitions. I was afraid of never seeing him again, and this fear somehow got bundled up with my fear of never seeing her again. What I was experiencing, for the first time in my life, was the torment of feeling forsaken by others and the despair that follows.

At sunset, I arrived at a bustling village. I learned from my innkeeper that I had traveled outside of the Licchavi kingdom and was in one of the villages of the neighboring Mallas. He also told me that a famous bhikkhu had arrived earlier in the day. This bhikkhu was going to give a discourse that night under the town's banyan tree. The thought of listening to one of Siddhattha's bhikkhus speak about the Dhamma lightened my heart and gave me something to look forward to. I ate, got settled in my room, and then went out to hear this renowned bhikkhu.

Night had fallen, the air was sweet, the town was alive with commerce and conversation, though there were far too many mosquitoes humming about and sticking their prickly beaks into my skin. Fortunately, there were fires and incense burning near the banyan tree to keep them away. The bhikkhu had not yet arrived. A respectable group of people were waiting for him, mostly middle-aged men who, as I could hear, loved to discuss philosophy. As I edged in closer to the tree, an elderly woman offered me a stool.

No sooner had I sat down, I heard horns approaching, first faintly and then louder. I looked up and saw a procession coming closer. There were several young men dressed in white walking proudly toward me. They were carrying a bhikkhu in an ornate chair above their shoulders. The bhikkhu was set down at the foot of the towering tree, right in front of me. His physical appearance reminded me of King Chetaka. His head hair and beard were shaved to the nubs and he appeared to have recently bathed. His robes were freshly dyed, washed, and pressed. His appearance was very presentable, so I smiled as a way of complimenting him on his looks. He looked away. Then he motioned to one of the young men to have his seat moved back, but after trying to push it over the tree roots and having it rock back and forth almost throwing him to the ground, he ordered the man to just leave it where it was. Then he gave me a hostile look, obviously meant to intimidate me.

This bhikkhu was not making a good impression. I was tempted to get up and leave. Then I remembered that a couple of weeks earlier two bhikkhus visited the Buddha to complain about the offensive conduct of a fellow bhikkhu. Could this be that bhikkhu? Was it Siha?

I tried to see beneath his outward appearance. His profile was stern. He possessed an air of confidence. There was probably no doubt in mind that whatever he said was right. He most certainly saw himself as superior to anyone else. But I knew the real story behind this bhikkhu. So, I intended to listen closely and memorize all that I could. Perhaps chronicling his words might help Siddhattha decide the fate of this self-important bhikkhu.

In a loud voice, he told everyone to be silent. Then he said, "Enlightenment is a fine gem, my friends. Come, see this gem, hear my words, and you shall be set free. I am Siha, a Great Sage who imparts the teaching the Buddha. Do not mistake me for an idle ignorant disciple, for I speak my own truth from my own realization. What is that truth?

"There is no self. Yes, that is so. There is no doer of an action, no enjoyer of a reward, no one who suffers on account of a misdeed. Since there is no self, all desire, all anger, all foolishness, is not owned by anyone, but just passes through the mind, arising and perishing each instant. With no self, I do not desire when desire comes over me, I do not hate when hatred comes over me, and I do not become a fool when foolish ideas enter my mind. That is one part of the freedom of no self.

"The other part is that nothing can cling to my consciousness. When I speak an untruth, it is said and gone. I have no remorse over what I have done. That is true freedom. All it takes is the view of no self. Now come with me. I am traveling to meet the Buddha, who has been wrongly told that I distort the Dhamma when I preach it exactly as it is. With many people by my side, he will be convinced that I speak the truth and am as fully enlightened as he."

He looked around the crowd for faces that showed agreement with his words, and when he spotted a believer, he motioned to one of his male servants to approach that individual and start up a conversation. Finally, his gaze settled on me. He felt so superior just then that he tried to stare me down. I was tempted to stand up and address the crowd, but instead I stayed calm and silently rose from my seat, returning to my room at the inn.

It was odd that I should witness this spectacle as a prelude to seeing Siddhattha one last time. I knew, with conviction, that Siha was not teaching the Buddha's Dhamma, though what he taught could sound like it. Perhaps that was the extent of my actual understanding of the Dhamma.

XXVIII

Leaving the Malla village before sunrise enabled me to catch up with Siddhattha and his bhikkhus just as they set up camp on the bank of a sparsely wooded stream.

I tied my horse to a tree and then made my way over to them. When I approached the stream, I saw the samanera who was sent to get me on the first morning of this long journey.

"Chronicler," he said, smiling, "where have you been? So much has happened. You must see Siddhattha at once. He has asked for you several times since your departure."

This baffled me. Why would Siddhattha, knowing that I was in Vesali, ask for me?

Siddhattha was seated a short distance from the other bhikkhus. The samanera left my side and I approached. At the appropriate distance, I bowed and looked up at him. His eyes were averted. I was not even sure he knew I was there. I sat down quietly to one side and waited.

Siddhattha's face looked tense. I had a strange feeling that a regular person, one who is filled with anger and dread, would burst forth out of the Buddha's body. But I was mistaken. The tenseness in his face was something else altogether.

"Chronicler, it is good you have joined us again. Forgive me if I am brief, for I am overcome by fever, weakness, and loose bowels. I have thought about your verses frequently and wish to hear you recite them in their entirety."

"I am sorry you are ill," I said.

"It will pass. With rain comes mosquitoes, and from them comes the fever. There is nothing that brings only good, only harm. The good of today may be the source of future conflict or peace. No one knows. We need not know that to become fully liberated. Please, recite your verses."

I hesitated for a few moments, repeating the whole poem once in my mind to make sure I had it perfectly memorized. I cleared my throat twice, and with some noticeable tension in my vocal cords, I began to recite:

"From what source do arguments,
Disputes, sorrow, and envy arise?
Tell me about the source of pride,
Self-importance, and slander?

From holding something dear comes pride,
Arguments, disputes, sorrow, and envy.
Envy is connected with arguments and disputes,
While arguments give birth to slanderous words.

In the world, what is the origin of holding things dear
And the longings that get stirred up?
And what is the origin of the hope and the purpose of life
That people hold for their future?

A relentless hunger to be is the origin of holding things dear
And the longings that get stirred up in the world.
This is also the origin of the hope and the purpose
That people hold for their future.

What is the source of this relentless hunger to be?
From what source do judgments,

Anger, lies, and suspicions arise?
And those things spoken of by the sages?

This relentless hunger to be arises lifted up by the
	experiences of pleasure and pain in the world.
People are put into turmoil over decisive judgments
And the destruction and creation of what they see.
Anger, lies, suspicions, and those things sages speak of
	arise out of pleasure and pain.
One who doubts would learn,
Following the path of higher knowledge,
Having listened to the teachings of the Great Sage.

What is the source of pleasure and pain?
In the absence of what do these not become?
Tell me, from what source is creation and destruction?

The source of pleasure and pain involves the senses making
	contact with their objects.
In the absence of sense contact, pleasure and pain do not arise.
I tell you that it is from the mind touching the world that
	creation and destruction arise.

What is the source of contact in the world?
And how do possessions come to be?
In the absence of what does selfishness not arise?
In the extinguishing of what do our senses stop making contact?

Sense contact arises depending on the presence of a body
	and a mind.
Possessions have their source in the wishing for them.
When there is no wishing for anything,
There is no selfishness.
In the extinguishing of sensation, perception, and ideation,
The mind stops touching the world."

"Well said, Chronicler. You have added some insightful verses. Let this poem be taught to my bhikkhus, so that they may investigate how one thing comes to be dependent on another within their experience. But now, if you would allow me, I would like to add to your poem what only a Buddha can see and know."

Though he was ill, Siddhattha's mind was still extremely sharp.

"From what manner of investigating
Does sensation, perception, and ideation, along with happiness
        and sorrow vanish?
Tell me, by what path do these vanish?
My heart is set to make this known.

Not by being
Conscious of consciousness,
Conscious of altered consciousness,
Conscious of extinguished consciousness,
Or by being unconscious.
Sensation, perception, and ideation only vanish by
        investigating this:
The pervading imagination of self-existence as the source of
        consciousness."

I listened closely to his verses, committing them to memory, though my thoughts circled around what to make out of his praise for my poem. Did it mean that I was liberated? I had to ask him that right then and there.

"Would you not say that someone who can write such a poem, capturing your teaching without misinterpretation, is liberated?"

"Chronicler," he said, "you are not liberated. It is not your fault. There is a barrier around your heart that keeps liberation outside. You are truly divided within."

"Can you awaken my heart?"

"That is not how it works. The heart is already awake in those who become liberated from hearing the Dhamma. Your heart is still asleep. It is dreaming of an image of the young woman you have promised to marry. It will not awaken from this dream, not even after her physical form has perished. Be patient. Someday this dream will end and you will find that you can no longer live the life of a chronicler. That is when we will meet again."

I did see the Buddha the next day, however. He looked calm and refreshed, his illness gone. He also seemed unperturbed when Siha and his train of followers found us camped off the main road to Savatthi.

I had planned to leave for Rajagaha, but when I saw Siha, I knew I had to stay and see how Siddhattha was going to deal with him. My imagination conjured up a wide variety of punishments, though I knew full well, from my own experience, that his personal hell was his deluded, grandiose self. No one could punish him more harshly than his own kamma. Nonetheless, I wanted to hear how the Buddha would rebuke this arrogant bhikkhu and put him in his place.

Siha was not carried in the chair this time but walked at the head of his train of followers. When he reached the area where the bhikkhus had gathered, he had his followers set his chair down. To my surprise, he offered the chair to the Buddha and chose to sit on the ground.

It was an odd sight seeing the Buddha sitting in Siha's chair, while Siha sat below him, grinning as if he had won the Buddha over to his side. The Buddha, however, appeared unmoved by Siha's calculated gesture of respect and quickly got to the matter at hand.

"I have asked you here, Venerable Siha, to clear up reports regarding your conduct as a bhikkhu. Do you wish to speak first or hear these reports and respond to them?"

Siha said, "Let me hear what has been said about me first."

"As you wish," Siddhattha said. Then he looked over at me and said, "Chronicler, would you relate to this bhikkhu what the two bhikkhus said concerning him?"

When Siha recognized who I was, his face dropped.

I stepped forward and gladly repeated what I heard.

"Two bhikkhus came to see the Buddha and this is what they said: 'Soon after his going forth, Siha claimed that he was fully liberated. He persuaded some lay supporters in our village to build him a hut. When the hut was built, he asked them to build an assembly hall. When the hall was built, he asked them for a chair the size of a throne. When the chair was placed in the hall, he asked them to spread the word that Siha the Enlightened One would be speaking in his hall daily, and that everyone should come and give him offerings. For the first several days, laypeople from the surrounding villages came to see Siha. They asked him for all sorts of boons, and he refused none of them. Most of the people asked him for wealth or for a good marriage arrangement for a son or daughter, but one man asked to obtain the wife of another man for his bride, while another asked that an enemy of his be stricken with illness. These people gave money and jewels to Siha, who accepted them knowing that these riches were given as payment for their requests being fulfilled. Word spread that Siha did not have the magical powers he had led people to believe he possessed. Still, he accepted gifts and proclaimed that he was enlightened, which angered many of the villagers. People stopped coming to see him. His hall was empty. His anger grew. The villagers, who now feared and hated Siha, shut their doors and would not give alms to any bhikkhu. The Sangha was shunned, and so all of the bhikkhus in that part of Magadha left to join the virtuous bhikkhus that reside in Rajagaha.'"

Siddhattha remained still throughout my recounting, while Siha fidgeted. He wanted to interrupt me a couple of times. I continued speaking, ignoring him as completely as I could, concentrating on recollecting exactly what I had heard.

When I was finished, instead of defending himself, Siha deferred to the Buddha, who spoke next.

"Siha, now that you have heard all that was said about you, what do you have to say? Is it true or not? Or, is one part true and the rest false? What have you to say, please?"

Though Siha was ruffled, his speech was direct.

"There is some truth in what was recounted, but the rest is malicious and false."

"What would be the truth?"

Siha said, "It is true that my lay followers built me a hut, a hall, and a chair. It is also true that I say I am enlightened and believe that to be so. But it is false to say that I accepted gifts as payment for granting boons or that I pandered to the immoral wishes of some of my followers. I was not the cause of other bhikkhus not receiving alms in our village. It was their laziness and maligning of my good name that brought such misfortune upon them."

"I see," Siddhattha said. "The root of your behavior lies in your belief in being fully enlightened. You imagine yourself to be my equal, but you do not think nor act like my equal. You see yourself as being superior to everyone else around you. You are consumed by delusions born of the three-fold conceit: I am equal to, superior to, inferior to. One who is fully liberated has destroyed this conceit and uprooted its cause. Work on your own liberation, disband your following, and renounce the world of acquisition, fame, and self-importance."

Siha was stunned by what he had just heard. He must not have fully comprehended what the Buddha meant, for he jumped to his feet and began to plead with Siddhattha.

"But, Venerable Siddhattha," he said, "I know full well the teaching of no self. I have been illuminated by its wisdom and have brought that profound understanding to those who have listened attentively to my sermons."

The Buddha glanced at me and said, "Chronicler, recount the words you heard but two days ago, so that I may correct what is in error."

I hesitated for a couple of minutes, trying to recall exactly what Siha said in his discourse.

"He preached a doctrine that sounded like this: 'There is no self. There is no doer of an action, no enjoyer of a reward, no one who suffers on account of a misdeed. Since there is no self, all desire, all anger, all foolishness, is not mine but just passes through my mind, arising and perishing each instant. With no self, I do not desire when desire comes over me, I do not hate when hatred comes over me, and I do not become a fool when foolish ideas enter my mind. That is one part of the freedom of no self. The other part is that nothing can cling to my consciousness. When I speak an untruth, it is said and gone. I have no remorse over what I have done. That is true freedom. All it takes is the view of no self.'"

"Does that rightly convey what you teach, Venerable Siha?" The Buddha said.

Siha straightened his back and beamed with pride. He looked around at the faces of all the bhikkhus, as though he was expecting them to shower him with praise.

"Yes, that is exactly what I said."

"Then listen closely and learn from your errors. Higher understanding requires self-reflection, not self-abandonment. There is a doer of an action only in the sense that a doer is needed to feel remorse over wrong actions and joy over good actions. An enjoyer and sufferer are needed to see clearly within oneself the fruits of actions and to know what actions to avoid in the future. These are not real entities, but they are useful constructs. To believe in an absolute Doer, Sufferer, Enjoyer is to fall into delusion. But, to see with penetrating insight the conditioned and constructed nature of the doer, the enjoyer, the sufferer, that is wisdom.

"You believe that desire, anger, and foolishness just pass through your mind without leaving a residue. You are mistaken. Desire, anger, and foolishness have a home within you, and they will return whenever the proper conditions arise. That you view yourself as not having a self only gives desire, anger, and foolishness the fuel they need in order to survive indefinitely.

"Feel the pain that honest self-reflection digs up. Investigate the hidden root of that pain. Study how the root is fed and nurtured. Then you may discover how to uproot it. When that is done, come speak to us about liberation."

The Buddha got up from the chair and motioned to everyone that it is time to resume their journey to Savatthi. Siha's followers all left him, and he, sitting alone, wounded by what had happened, began to weep.

I knew that my time with the Buddha was now over. With the addition of Siddhattha's verses, my poem was complete, and so was my work. Now, I could return to Rajagaha, where I would present King Bimbisara with my poem, as well as recount to him what Siddhattha said to his disciples and to the public.

XXIX

Thirty years later, during King Ajatasattu's reign

Over thirty years have passed since I last saw Siddhattha. And now I am about to meet him again. Devadatta is pleased with my detailed description of Nataputta's way of life. Though once in his employ, I may never be able to get free of him. He has granted my family their freedom, but he still wants me to do something he believes only I can do.

It seems that Devadatta has alienated everyone who is close to the Buddha. He cannot find anyone he trusts who the Buddha also trusts, leaving only me. Nataputta's prophecy that I would help Devadatta kill the Buddha appears to be coming true. And now he has ordered me, on the threat of death, because otherwise I would not be giving in as easily as I am, to go at once to the town of Nalanda and wait for his assassins to arrive. He assures me that I will recognize the assassins. I shall then bring them to the Buddha. That is all I have to do. Yet, I also suspect he does not genuinely trust me, for I am not to be trusted.

One thing about Devadatta's plot that pleases me is that I will get to see the Buddha again. Perhaps I can pick up where I left off thirty years ago. Inspired by the thought of being in the Buddha's presence tomorrow, I compose my own closing verses to my poem:

You have told us that which we have asked.
And now we ask you to explain one more thing.
Do some sages say that godlike purity is only so much?
Or do they say it is other than this?

Some believe it is only so much,
But there are others who believe in a time when a good state
*   of mind appears*
That does not succumb to illusions.
Knowing all beliefs to be supported by thought,
The sage who investigates,
Studying the causes of views,
With this knowledge is liberated.
He does not dispute with others
Nor is he drawn into one existence after another.

XXX

When in the present moment, I am confused. The present brings me to my feelings, an inner bubbling of indecision, remorse, and stifled passions. There is nothing to chronicle, nothing someone else would want to hear. There is only the chaos of not knowing what the present moment is beyond the turning and tumbling of my emotions. I have asked myself this question, buried at times beyond recognition over the past thirty years: How do the sages see clearly in the present? Are they not caught in this very same chaos? Or do they truly know the end of all this turning and tumbling?

I am with my father today, hoping for his return to consciousness, yet anticipating his last breath. I must speak to my father one last time and tell him what I have hidden in my heart these past three decades. Perhaps all I need to do is to hear myself say it, for it seems that I am using his impending death as an excuse to tell him my secret. So, I kneel by his bed, my face near his, my lips almost touching his right ear.

I whisper, "Father, I have a secret to tell you. I have honored you and have never failed to keep your view of life alive within me. You were present in all of my decisions. Even though I knew it was but an image of you, for me it was who you are. Before you die, I must speak the secret by which your image will die within me. Too long have I battled with your ghost and conceded to its superior strength. Now, I must rise to claim the path of my heart.

"The secret is this: I shall, once I have averted the attempt on Siddhattha's life, renounce the world and live as a bhikkhu."

There, I have said it. His eyes grow dull at my revelation. I do not know if he heard me, but more importantly, I have made a promise to myself.

Over three decades ago, when I left Siddhattha to return to Rajagaha, I rode alone for several days, only speaking briefly with strangers when I stopped for food and rest. I had no companion, no one to talk to, except the inner voices I would create for the sake of dialog. One such voice was my father's. To my father, I spoke of my joy at having found a woman who loved me. And, I enumerated all the wonderful prospects that would arise for me upon becoming known as King Bimbisara's Chronicler. In my imagination, my father's joy was exaggerated, as was his pride. I had arrived as an adult and was to be an important man in the world, carrying on the family tradition of serving the king. I would rise above my peers and be recognized as the foremost chronicler of the court. My destiny was to be fulfilled. This would be the best life I could ever hope to achieve.

The other voice was Siddhattha's. To Siddhattha, I spoke of my fears of married life and the burdensome obligations of being King Bimbisara's Chronicler. Siddhattha's voice was compassionate, yet firm about the dangers of living in the world and how I would not stay with the rudiments of the Dhamma. He knew I would remember his words while forgetting what he taught as the true path to nibbana. I was the worst kind of gifted student. The one who memorizes and studies everything the teacher says, but does not apply that teaching in the way that it was meant.

The wisdom inherent in Siddhattha's words burrowed into the honeycomb of my heart, but was sapped by the pleasing hopes and fantasies my mind so eagerly pursued. Every third year or so, during a time when fear and restlessness arose to consume my being with their fever, the wisdom of Siddhattha's words would trickle out to soothe the fear and disperse the restlessness. Remembering Siddhattha's words would bring meaning to my experience and add to my knowledge, though mere words were unable to alter my path. I could sense that recollecting someone else's wisdom was not enough to liberate me from my anguish. Someday, I would have to cultivate my own wisdom.

Now I believe that day has come. My heart is ready to awaken to the Dhamma. I can hear my heart speaking in one voice, recalling the words of a young Licchavi prince at his ordination:

"I go forth in the teaching of Siddhattha, where wisdom arises in the freedom from sorrow. I shall from this day on walk in Siddhattha's shadow to Siddhattha's light."

XXXI

I say farewell to my brother, his wife, and his children. They cry and beg me to stay. I am also saddened by my departure, much more so than I believed possible. My tears make it hard for me to see as I walk through town in the direction of Nalanda.

Once I am outside the city gates, a new fear takes hold of my mind. I must warn the Buddha that two soldiers have been sent to kill him. If I would have left yesterday, as Devadatta had instructed, I would now be with the Buddha and could warn him before the assassins arrive.

Since I am on foot, having given up my worldly possessions, which includes my horse, I have no other choice but to run to Nalanda. I arrive exhausted, panting in the late afternoon heat. I decide to stop at an inn and get a meal before I search for the assassins.

At the inn, I sit at a table and order a plate of food. I see two men at a nearby table who look like soldiers. When they notice me looking at them, they come over to my table.

One of them is a huge man with a round bearded face and a friendly smile. The other reminds me of King Ajatasattu. He is very thin and has a strained look. He glares at me often as we speak.

The thin soldier says, "All of Siddhattha's bhikkhus wear the same colored robes, shave their heads, and move about quietly. If you had not appeared, we might have killed an innocent man."

"You will kill an innocent man if you go ahead with this."

The bearded soldier, annoyed by my remark, says, "You do not want us to kill Siddhattha? Then why did our king send you as our guide?"

I am confused by this comment. "King Ajatasattu has sent you? Not Devadatta?"

The thin soldier replies, "Our captain has sent us, saying that our orders came directly from King Ajatasattu. That is good enough for us."

The other man heartily agrees. They both stare at me, waiting for me to chime in that it is good enough for me too. Fortunately, I can think for myself.

"Is this the extent of the plot that was told to you? Nothing more was revealed?" I ask.

The bearded soldier says, "Our orders are to stab Siddhattha several times until we are sure he is dead."

The thin one adds, "And then flee by the road we came."

Devadatta's plot instantly becomes clear to me.

"Then you do not know that a trap has been set. For neither King Ajatasattu nor Devadatta wants anyone to know that the Buddha's death was their doing. They will have you killed, just as they will have me killed. But if do not kill Siddhattha and then take a different road than previously arranged, all of us shall live."

The thin one's fierce stare intensifies. He then asks, "How do you know we will be killed? Who told you this?"

"No one had to tell me. To Devadatta, our lives are expendable. He wants the Buddha dead, but he cannot be the one who kills him. Think of what he has to lose if someone found out that he was the one who had the Buddha killed. No one would ever believe he is a true sage."

"You are right," the thin one says. "He would be known as a murderer."

"Right!" I say. "So, Devadatta must have everyone who knows of this plot killed. Then we will be blamed for it!"

My words are having a tremendous effect. They are silent, thinking to themselves. The thin soldier has a fretful look.

He asks his partner, "What should we do?"

"Come with me," I say. "I will introduce you to the Buddha. He has compassion for everyone, even those who have meant him harm."

The huge, bearded man says defiantly, "I will never become a sage! I am a soldier!"

The other soldier says, "Our only option is to leave the service of our king and join the service of another."

"Then I will help you find employment with King Pasenadi of Kosala, who is ever grateful for my service as King Bimbisara's Chronicler. Would that be suitable?"

They enthusiastically embrace my proposal. I am very pleased with myself for having the courage to stop the assassination of my teacher. One thing I learned from my brahmin teachers was to never betray a worthy teacher and always protect him from harm. Such noble action pleases the gods and creates happiness in the human realm.

XXXII

I surmised that the Buddha would be staying at the monastery originally built by Siha's lay supporters in Nalanda, not far from the northern boundary of the town. I walk in that direction after making sure that the two soldiers know what to say to King Pasenadi upon their arrival in Savatthi.

I feel elated, but not for long. I begin to imagine Devadatta's reaction upon hearing the news that his plot has failed. Fear begins to gnaw at me and soon I am trembling. I know I can never go back to Rajagaha, for I would be imprisoned on the spot. I might not be safe in Nalanda, or in any of the towns and villages in Magadha, at least until Devadatta no longer has influence over King Ajatasattu. My plan is to see the Buddha, receive his blessing, and be ordained as a bhikkhu. Then I could walk to Savatthi without being recognized. Once there, I can ask King Pasenadi for asylum.

As a bhikkhu, even King Ajatasattu will most likely have to pardon me, just as King Pasenadi pardoned the mass murderer Angulimala after he became a bhikkhu. But King Pasenadi resented the Buddha for ordaining Angulimala instead of handing him over to the king's guards. The Buddha then made a rule that fugitives from the law could not be ordained as bhikkhus.

Then again, I have not committed any crime but prevented one. The Buddha would probably see my course of action as bearing good fruit, even though I tricked the two soldiers.

But did I lie to them? It is conceivable that Devadatta had planned to kill the three of us after the Buddha was confirmed dead. Otherwise, why would he have ordered them to leave by the same road? Perhaps he has sent other soldiers to assassinate the assassins. Such a plot could easily be executed by Devadatta.

Still, I am in turmoil as I walk to the monastery, though no longer over whether I am a criminal, for I have absolved myself of any crime. Instead, I am uncertain about handing my life over to Siddhattha, worried about how I will survive. I am afraid of the forest and do not like the idea of begging for food. What if I become ill? Will there be no one to take care of me? Do bhikkhus just let each other wither away in times of illness? What if I end up starving to death without having arrived at nibbana?

This is the longest walk in my life. Twice I consider turning back, badgered by a sense of duty to return to my ailing father, so that I may be near him when he dies. Fortunately, my feet keep moving forward. I let my body lead and find that my fears come and go.

I arrive at the monastery at dusk. The resident bhikkhus appear to have retired to their rooms. I find the Buddha in the assembly hall that was built for Siha. Siddhattha has aged gracefully, looking much as he did when I last saw him thirty years ago. He is meditating while sitting in Siha's chair. At first I decide not to disturb him, but then it occurs to me that he could never feel disturbed, so I gently place my hand on his right shoulder. Slowly his eyes open and his presence animates his body. He recognizes me instantly.

"Chronicler, you have finally appeared. Is your heart united?"

"Yes, my heart now speaks in one voice. Will you accept me into your Sangha?"

"I have but to say, 'Come, Padipa, be a lamp unto yourself, and from this day forward live as a bhikkhu in the Buddha's Sangha,' and it is done."

I bow to the Buddha. Then I ask, "Where will I find a set of robes and a bowl? Where will I sleep?"

He replies, "You no longer have any cares. All will be taken care of."

"I have forgotten so many of your teachings that I do not know what to do now."

"Then recall what teachings you can. That is all you need."

"But what do I do?" I ask, desperately.

"Nothing. Absolutely nothing. Free yourself from doing."

"I still do not know what to do!" I say, unable to understand what he means.

"Be still and all will become known."

I am more bewildered than ever before. Has Siddhattha become vague and mysterious over these past three decades? This is not the Siddhattha I knew before. But then again, I am not the man I was before either.

XXXIII

I find a room in the monastery and sleep soundly through the night. When I awake at dawn, I am startled by all the noise. Bhikkhus are washing up, raking leaves, and conversing with each other not far from my room. Two bhikkhus knock on my door and welcome me as if I were a long-lost friend. They offer to bring me a set of robes and shave my head. Today, I have no hesitation at the thought of becoming a bhikkhu. Instead, I feel as though I have finally found my true calling.

After I put on the mendicant robes, they shave my head. Now that I look like a bhikkhu, I must find the Buddha and thank him for allowing me to join his Sangha. He is not where I saw him the previous night, so I begin to look for him. In my search for Siddhattha, I ask several of the bhikkhus if they know where he is. The odd thing about this situation is that not a single one of them seems to know that the Buddha is staying here. They make it sound as if I was dreaming the night before. But then, how would the two bhikkhus have known that I was to have taken robes that morning unless the Buddha had told them? When I look for them, they too are nowhere to be found.

This makes me feel terribly alone. The friendliness of the twenty or so bhikkhus living here does nothing to take away my confusion. What am I to do? How am I to spend my time? I feel like a little boy for having these concerns. I am angry at myself for needing someone to tell me what to do. But, instead of asking the bhikkhus what I should do, I try to observe them and follow their example.

I am given an alms bowl by an elderly monk who appears to be the senior-most bhikkhu. He tells me to avoid the center of town on my alms round. That is all the instruction I get. I do not know how to ask for alms. Do I just go up to a person and ask him to fill my bowl with food? No. I begin to remember how the bhikkhus did it thirty years ago. They would keep their eyes on the ground in front of them and go up to a house. They would stand outside of the house and wait for someone to come outside and bring them food. They would be completely silent, accepting the food they got.

That is exactly what I set out to do. I walk barefoot in my brown robe with my freshly shaven head exposed to the hot morning sun. I do not feel like my old self anymore. I would never have done this out of choice. But this is what bhikkhus do.

I stop in front of a big house. I stand there in plain sight. I see people sitting and talking on the porch, not paying any attention to me. I feel a surge of rage at being ignored, at being a failure, at the painful thought that I will not eat today because these people are too caught up in their own lives to help a starving sage. Minutes pass and still no one goes into the house to get food for me. My anger at these wealthy, stingy people grows. The merit they would gain by giving me food is worth a hundred times the food they give. Do they not know that?

A few more minutes pass. Instead of my rage and impatience growing, I become saddened by the fact that these people do not care about giving alms to bhikkhus. They have apparently decided not to honor bhikkhus with offerings of food. It is their choice, and it is not my responsibility to change that. Now that I am a bhikkhu, I must live with what I get from people. And, if I receive neglect, then I will have to learn to live with that, even if it means not eating.

The next house is smaller than the first, but still big enough for an extended family. As soon as I stop to stand in front of it, a young girl comes out with some food wrapped in leaves. She is a shy child and is afraid to get too close to me. Her mother's voice reaches her ears, telling her that I am a bhikkhu and will not harm her. The girl comes closer. She peers into my empty bowl, lowering the wrapped leaves gently to the bottom. Then she jumps back, looks at me for a second with a spark of light in her eyes, giggling as she darts back inside.

I smile at the girl's mother. If I was allowed to thank her, I would. But that is not done by bhikkhus. We take our food without giving thanks to those who feed us. Now I understand why. The whole interaction is blessed with a happiness beyond words. I then recall that I have never given alms to any sage, though I was rarely at my house during the day. If a bhikkhu had shown up on my doorstep while I was there, silently waiting for me to bring him food, would I have put anything in his alms bowl? I am not sure.

I return to the monastery and eat in my room. Afterward, I resist the urge to take a nap and instead decide to work on finding liberation from suffering and rebirth. A long time ago, in a cave beneath Vulture Peak, Siddhattha said that recollection would be my path. I now construe that to mean that I am to use my excellent memory.

I go to the hall where I saw Siddhattha the night before and sit on a mat with my back touching the wall. I picture the Buddha sitting here in front of me. "Be still," Siddhattha says, "and all will become known." I contemplate these words, arriving at a vague feeling that all I need to know is within me, but I cannot see.

I cannot see. This thought brings my attention back to sitting with my eyes closed. It is true that I cannot see. That is an undeniable truth about my experience right now. What else is true?

I sit with my back touching the wall. My body is breathing. It is true that I breathe. If I were not breathing, I would be dead. Breathing is a necessary part of living. It may be the life force, but there does not need to be anything special about it. It can simply be a truth of my experience.

Is this what the Buddha meant when he said, "Be still and all will become known"? Thirty years ago, I would have tried to answer that question. Today, I let it dissolve while I keep still.

Over the course of my first few weeks as a bhikkhu, my mind has been unusually dull and apathetic. I think that is because I have tried to make it become still. I have only felt truly awake when I recount the wise words, good deeds, and exemplary tales of the Buddha, his bhikkhus, and the gravest of sages, Nataputta. But such recollections eventually give way to other thoughts; before I know it, I am lost in a fantasy of how today's meal will taste, the nap afterward, and the end of another day.

After about four months, a fellow bhikkhu asks me to go with him to see the Buddha in Savatthi. I suddenly remember that before I had grown so comfortable here in Nalanda, I was planning to stay in Savatthi. But since King Ajatasattu has sent no one to apprehend me, and I am for all appearances free to do as I please, I have just stayed put. Now I see that if I am going to break free of my current lethargy, I need to embark on a pilgrimage.

During the long journey to Savatthi, my memories of thirty years ago come back in a way I have never experienced before. I always remember what someone says. I hear his words in his own voice. As I listen, I can then speak those same words. My mind keeps that person's voice alive. But now it is not the person's voice that is kept alive in memory, but the person's mind. It often happens with the Buddha's voice these days, as if his mind somehow lives inside my consciousness.

One afternoon, we stop by the same stream where I recited my poem to Siddhattha and received his praise. I decide to sit under the very same tree where the Buddha added his verses to my poem. My mind recalls him telling me what only a Buddha can see and know.

"Not by being
Conscious of consciousness,
Conscious of altered consciousness,
Conscious of extinguished consciousness,
Or by being unconscious.
Sensation, perception, and ideation only vanish by
investigating this:
The pervading imagination of self-existence as the source of
consciousness."

I close my eyes and settle in to the stillness of my body. It does not take long for my mind to dislodge the chronicler self.

At that moment, I glimpse what a Buddha knows.

And, in the next moment, I know how a Buddha sees.

EPILOGUE

Three years later, during King Ajatasattu's reign

I have been living in Savatthi these past three years and have
recently returned to Rajagaha. Much has gone on in the world
since I left it. The stories and rumors reach the monasteries as
fast as anywhere else, and there are bhikkhus, such as myself,
who pay attention to the news of wars, of kingdoms expanding
and falling, of highway murderers and thieves being caught and
executed, and of the funerals of famous teachers.

I am happy to say that in the last three years the world has
turned around, though not without its share of subterfuge and
violence. Devadatta's story is a good example. He was feared
by many, including myself, and now he is dead. He gave up on
hiring assassins, for they really could not be trusted. Instead, he
attempted to kill the Buddha by pushing a boulder down a hill
while the Buddha was walking below. Luckily, the Buddha's leg
was only grazed by the boulder, leaving him with a slight but
noticeable limp. Then Devadatta made use of the information
I gave him about Nataputta's way of life, twisting Nataputta's
determination to harm no living being to suit his own purpose.
Devadatta was able to create dissension in the Sangha by raising
the point that the Buddha allowed the consumption of meat,
arguing that, under any circumstance, eating meat was improper
for a true sage. Through this schism in the Sangha, Devadatta
acquired a few followers who stayed with him in a monastery
donated by King Ajatasattu. Not long after that, he died.

King Ajatasattu, meanwhile, put his attention on conquest,
setting his sights very high. He fought King Pasenadi of Kosala,
on four separate occasions, being the victor in the first three
battles, losing the fourth. He was taken prisoner in an ambush.
I have heard that King Ajatasattu's imprisonment had a sobering
effect on his pride. His uncle released him on the condition that
he would never attack Kosala again.

Today, King Ajatasattu wishes to meet the Buddha. It is
rumored that the king has a special question, one that he has

posed to several renowned sages. Not convinced by their answers, he now wishes to hear what the Buddha will say. I plan to be there, but not as a chronicler, for I have long abandoned that old self, but as one who still seeks to see and know as the Buddha sees and knows.

After the morning meal, all the bhikkhus gather in Jivaka's mango grove to confess their transgressions to each other. When they are done, the Buddha addresses the community of bhikkhus regarding King Ajatasattu's visit.

"King Ajatasattu will arrive shortly in the grand fashion he is accustomed to. There will be elephants, soldiers, and many women of the palace here in Jivaka's mango grove. The world of power and wealth will descend upon us, to visit us, to learn from us, but not to entice any of us back into its sphere. Those of you who fear that such contact will disrupt your learning, or tempt your senses, take care to find a place away from here where you can be restrained and at peace."

Several bhikkhus leave the mango grove. About a hundred of us remain, waiting for King Ajatasattu's arrival. In the distance, I can hear the palace elephants approaching. As they near, the ground starts to shake and the mango trees sway. I am standing not far from the wooden platform where the Buddha sits cross-legged, apparently unaffected by the tremors and commotion caused by King Ajatasattu's grand entrance.

Soldiers come into the grove and form a circle around the bhikkhus on the periphery. Then some officers order the bhikkhus who were blocking their way to move aside, so that they can make an aisle. Several boys come through and sweep the ground, making the aisle clean and safe to walk upon. I see King Ajatasattu approach us with his physician, Jivaka, the owner of this grove. Behind King Ajatasattu are many women of the palace, all dressed gaily as though they are on a pleasure outing. The Buddha was right. Their world has descended upon us. I can see why he prepared us beforehand.

Jivaka, a wise old man, who is the most revered physician in all of Magadha, singles out the Buddha for King Ajatasattu, who then mounts the platform and walks up to the Buddha, kneeling before him. Jivaka and the women of the court also approach and kneel. As they rise, servants place chairs on the platform, and each person in the king's entourage is led to a chair and offered a cushion.

Although I witnessed this type of spectacle countless times when I was King Bimbisara's Chronicler, for the first time the fuss and pomp struck me as absurd and sad. Already, the stage is set for all these people to use up the Buddha's time. I cannot imagine that any of them are actually ready to hear the Dhamma. But, then again, was I when I first met the Buddha?

An air of silence hangs over the grove for no more than a minute. King Ajatasattu rises from his seat and raises his voice so that everyone can hear.

"Tell me, Siddhattha Gotama, people do all sorts of work in this world and each kind of work produces some visible fruit. Now those who are sages, do they also do some work that produces some visible fruit?"

I do not ponder the question as much as wonder about the man who asked it. He truly doubts whether anything comes from taking up a spiritual path and following it. I was of the same mind once. It now strikes me as immature for a man to ask about a way of life, whether it is worthwhile or not, if it is impossible for him to ever take up that way of life.

Before replying to King Ajatasattu's question, the Buddha asks the king to tell him how the other sages have answered this very same question. My mind goes elsewhere, for I know within myself the fruits of the sage's life.

As I look around at the other bhikkhus, wondering what some of them might be thinking, I see a samanera not more than twelve years old with a look on his face that I know all too well. He is memorizing the Buddha's words.

Suddenly, I see myself at his age. The dreamlike fabric of my entire life bursts into consciousness and I see my self-existence as a knot rapidly untying itself until there is nothing left but a heap of threads.

The future does not belong to those who attain nibbana, for they have passed beyond it, but to those who chronicle the Dhamma and hand it down to future generations.

Now, my work is done.

After
the
Parinibbana

Jason Siff

I

My ordained name is Sujata, one who is born fortunate, though I prefer to think of myself as being born in fortunate times. I am perhaps the last person alive who has heard the Buddha speak. That was over sixty years ago, not far from the temple that has been my home for all these years, situated on the outskirts of the town of Kusinara. Not far from my hermitage is where the Buddha became deathly ill and spoke to a group of us the day of his passing into parinibbana.

I was ordained as a samanera when I was twelve years old. My parents were lay followers of the Buddha and wanted me to join the Sangha. They had hoped that I would become an arahant and leave the beginningless cycle of death and rebirth, which the Buddha referred to as samsara. If they were alive today, I fear they would be disappointed by my lack of spiritual attainment, though they might be pleased by my feats of memorization. Many years ago, I knew all of the Buddha's discourses by heart and could recite them at will. But not so today.

The first speech of the Buddha's that I tried to memorize was one that was later recounted by Venerable Ananda at the congregation of arahants after the Buddha's parinibbana, where it was placed in a collection of longer discourses. I was affected by the whole event, not just the Buddha's speech, for King Ajatasattu of Magadha was present, with his wives and ministers, filling Jivaka's mango grove with the splendor of the royal court.

King Ajatasattu asked the Buddha, "Those who are sages, do they also do some kind of work that produces visible fruit?"

The Buddha then asked if he had posed this question to any of the other teachers in his realm. King Ajatasattu said that he had and then went on to explain their answers, for the king was acquainted with the spiritual teachers in his kingdom and the doctrines they professed.

He spoke at length of the teacher, Purana Kassapa, and what that sage taught. It was a doctrine of no responsibility for any action, as I understood it. In short, "If one kills, or causes to kill, another being, one does no evil." He also believed that there is no such thing as gaining merit in the world, so self-mastery and good deeds are of no use. I did not care for what I was hearing, but I continued to memorize all that I heard.

The next teacher King Ajatasattu spoke of was Makkhali Gosala, a naked ascetic whose family made him live in the cowshed as a child, and who was well known for his irreverent behavior. He believed that self-purification happens at a destined time in one's journey through samsara and that it does not matter if one practices restraint, self-awareness, good actions, or engages in the deeper states of meditation. In fact, Makkhali Gosala said, "The foolish and the wise, having roamed and wandered through various forms of existence, will alike make an end to suffering."

Then the king spoke of a teacher who believed that a person is made up of the four elements only and that there is nothing that exists after death. Therefore, this life is the only one there is. I found such a doctrine frightening, for if one believed in it, besides there being no heavenly or hellish realms of rebirth, much less rebirth in the human realm, there could be no such thing as the liberation of mind attained by the Buddha.

Then he spoke of an obscure teacher who proclaimed a doctrine of seven bodies (the four elements, pleasure, pain, and the soul), and that there is no doer or enjoyer of an action. These seven bodies are believed to be permanent, stable, and whole. According to King Ajatasattu, this teacher said that if someone were to behead another with a sword, he would not be taking that person's life, for the sword merely passes through the space between the seven bodies.

Then, the king spoke of his meeting with Nataputta, who, in his usual brevity, simply said, "The fruit of the sage's life arises from adhering to the four-fold restraint of the Jains."

The last teacher the king asked this question of was Sanjaya the skeptic. Sanjaya's way of looking at things was similar to the Buddha's, in that he questioned all assertions. He skirted the question by saying that he is not a person who says, "it is this way," "it is that way," "it is otherwise," "it is not so," or "it is not not so." He was the only teacher who did not proclaim a doctrine, though it was rumored he believed in living a quiet and peaceful life.

After King Ajatasattu related what these teachers said about the fruits of the sage's life, the Buddha gave his well-considered teaching on the benefits of living as a bhikkhu or *bhikkhuni*. He said many things that are better stated in Venerable Ananda's recounting than in my own. When I reflect back on what was said that day, I can see that I have lived the sage's life and known some of its fruits. I have not attained nibbana, nor have I experienced the higher knowledges and exalted states of consciousness, but I have lived a life free from inflicting harm on others, and on myself, which I attribute to following the monastic discipline set forth by the Buddha.

Thus, from the age of twelve to that of eighty-one, I have known the fruits of self-restraint. As my life nears its end, the question of the next life occupies my mind. Where will I be reborn? How might I secure a birth in the realm of the gods?

II

All of my students have been in the prime of their life when they met me. Some of them joined the Sangha at a tender age like I did, but most enter the Sangha after their nineteenth birthday. They have generally tasted something of worldly pleasure and misery before deciding to embark on this life. One such person is the bhikkhuni who comes to me every day for her lessons in the Dhamma. She is twenty years old, having joined the Sangha but a year ago. Her preceptor gave her one of those new colorful names that have become so popular. She is called, Padmapani, "Lotus Hand," which has a peculiar sensual quality to it, suited to her handsome face and bright eyes, but out of place for someone devoted to studying the Buddha's path to nibbana. Perhaps I am just old-fashioned, my head too full of our sacred lore, to accept the new names, the new ideas, the new leaning towards making the Dhamma pleasing for the masses. I would prefer it if she took the name of a venerated bhikkhuni, such as Mahapajapati, after the Buddha's stepmother, who was courageous, determined, and wise, without whom there would be no Bhikkhuni Sangha.

The Buddha was visiting his birthplace, Kapilavatthu. While staying outside of Kapilavatthu in the Nigrodha Grove, his step-mother, Mahapajapati, whose husband had already died and whose only son had joined the Sangha, thus bereft of family, had decided it was fit for her to enter the Sangha. The Buddha refused her request, not once, but thrice. She left in tears, and the Buddha left shortly thereafter for Vesali. Then Mahapajapati, determined to become a sage, cut off her hair and put on the robes of a bhikkhu. She journeyed to Vesali, where, at the entrance of the Buddha's residence, with swollen feet from walking such a long distance, tearful and in pain, she met Venerable Ananda, the Buddha's attendant. Ananda, whose skill in discourse and compassion were widely known, interceded on her behalf and the Buddha acquiesced to the inclusion of women in the Sangha. The Blessed One then made Mahapajapati (and every bhikkhuni after her) promise to observe additional precepts and also made them subordinate to the men in the Bhikkhu Sangha. Afterwards, the Buddha remarked to Ananda that because he let women join the Sangha, the life of the Dhamma would be cut in half and would thus only endure for five hundred years. In this regard, the Buddha said, "Households with many women, and few men, can easily fall prey to attackers and thieves."

The younger bhikkhus consider me to be conservative, but if they only knew how radical it once was for a bhikkhu to give instruction to a bhikkhuni, then they might think differently.

If they could just understand how circumspect the Sangha was when the Buddha was alive, they would see me as orthodox and wise; but instead, my knowledge is considered dated, and my counsel is seldom sought. The only person who seems to value my words is Padmapani. She even asks me for advice regarding problems she has with her fellow bhikkhunis. That she looks up to me as her spiritual teacher, holding me in such high esteem, makes me feel bitterness toward the bhikkhu who named her. Perhaps I can persuade her to change her name to Mahapajapati. Then she would be readily identified as one who prefers the teachings of the elders.

But this a fantasy, an old man's wish to have progeny where there is none. She is not my daughter, but my student, my laundress, and the one who brings me water and cleans my hut. Away from me, she is her own person, responsible for her own choices, no matter what kind of guidance I give her. We bhikkhus train ourselves to view relationships as temporary periods of learning, or passing on learning, and so do not become attached to people. But I fear, with her, I have already created such a deep and lasting attachment, that when my time comes, her image will occupy my last thought. Alas, one more factor affecting my next rebirth, increasing the odds that I will reborn a human, or worse yet, an animal, a hungry ghost, or an unfortunate soul lost in a realm of severe, unrelenting torment.

III

I spend all my time in and around my hut. It is a small mud hut with a few head-sized holes for windows, though more often someone peers through them to check on me than I peer out of them to look at the trees and bushes outside. The floor is clay with a straw mat for me to sleep on and stump of wood for me to sit on when I teach. My students bring their own mats.

The reason I seldom leave my hut has to do with my limited strength. Though I am not ill, my chest hurts, and my breathing becomes rough when I exert myself. The only time I walk a distance is on each *uposatha* day. On that day, arriving every full moon and new moon, a samanera shaves my head and beard, while Padmapani washes my extra set of robes and sweeps the path leading from my hut to the hermitage's meeting house.

Whenever Padmapani comes to me for her lesson, she must be accompanied by a man, who must be present throughout the time she is alone with me. Lately, a young man about her age has been joining her. He is her brother or cousin, for there is some resemblance, at least in physical features. But whereas she is gentle, thoughtful, and self-conscious, he is brash, argumentative, and holds a high opinion of himself. He certainly makes it hard for me to enjoy every moment of her company; which, I guess, makes him a good choice for the role he must play in our complex system of rules. Still, I wonder if he gets anything out of these lessons except more proof that elders like me are just old fools.

His name is Kunika, the true name of King Ajatasattu, and he appears emulate his namesake. Kunika's father is one of the local chieftains of the Malla clan, who once ruled Kusinara, but now are vassals to the Nanda kings of Magadha, heirs of the expansion carried out by King Ajatasattu, but no relation to him.

This Kunika is a tall, muscular, handsome man, who is as skilled at war games as he is at mind games. He aspires to be a great leader and may someday lead his people out from under tyranny, however small their numbers be, however insignificant the town of Kusinara is. For no one comes to Kusinara except pilgrims paying homage to the Buddha's remains, as the Malla's of Kusinara took the lion's share of Buddha's charred bones and teeth, which were later buried in a large mound not far from this hermitage.

That day, more than sixty years ago, when the Buddha stopped near this very hermitage, his body weak and pale, is clearly etched in my memory. Venerable Ananda, who was not cautious about what he said and to whom, let it be known in the town of Kusinara that the Buddha was dying. The townspeople flocked to see the Buddha, eager to receive his final blessing and hear his parting words. All the bhikkhus were equally curious, and a group of us begged Venerable Ananda to let us sit with the Buddha in his hut. Ananda was angry at himself for the turmoil his thoughtless speech had caused, so he refused entry to all who pleaded with him. The Buddha, however, could hear our pleas, and so granted us an audience. There were but ten us that could fit into the small mud hut, which was not much bigger than my own. We sat around the Buddha. His eyes were watery, yet they shone with the radiance of inner wisdom. He spoke slowly, trying to be as clear as possible.

He told us, "It might be that some of you think that now we have no Master, the Master's instruction has vanished. It should not be seen thus. What I have taught as the Dhamma and the rules of conduct will be your Master upon my parting."

Then he asked if anyone present was uncertain about specific points of the Dhamma. We kept silent, agreeing in our silence not to tax the Buddha's strength, so that he may live a few hours longer. When he asked again, I felt the impulse to speak, but then looked around at the sadness erupting on each face and decided to hold my tongue. Then he asked again, and I heard not his question but my heart aching at the thought of his passing from this world. Later that day, the Buddha addressed this same question to a large assembly of bhikkhus and bhikkhunis, meeting them outside of his hut. They kept silent as we did. To us, he bade us leave. To the assembly, he added, "Perhaps you do not ask out of respect for me. Then let one friend tell it to another." Still, no one communicated his or her doubts. Everyone kept silent. Like me, they were probably on the brink of some unimaginable grief.

The Buddha then said something that struck me as a decline in his faculties, normal for a man of eighty-one years, as I now know for myself. Because no one asked him to explain specific points of the Dhamma, he said that everyone present must have certain knowledge of the Dhamma and were destined for nibbana. I was sure about what I heard and even more sure that I did not have the knowledge he spoke of. When I looked around me, I could see that there were bhikkhus who nodded with agreement, bhikkhus who felt embarrassed, and bhikkhus who smiled with a self-important smirk.

When I returned my attention to the Buddha, he was already giving his final teaching.

"Conditioned things decay and die," he said. "Work diligently for your own liberation."

Then he closed his eyes, and everyone swarmed around him, trying to see if he was still alive. Ananda, who was nearest to the Buddha, opened his eyes and looked inside. He announced that the Buddha passed through the higher realms of subtle incorporeal existence to where he could not be found. In other words, the Buddha had completely abandoned samsara and entered parinibbana.

I was so struck with anguish that my legs trembled. It felt as though the whole Earth shook with grief. The Buddha was gone. Never to return.

This kind of recollection is extremely taxing for me these days. In the past, I could recall such events for hours on end without feeling the slightest fatigue. But now, after several minutes of seemingly effortless recollection, I feel sleep coming upon me. Or is it death?

IV

A woman's voice says not far from my ears, "Venerable Sujata! Venerable Sujata!"

Then a man says, "He is just sleeping. You'll wake him."

My eyes open and I see the blurry figure of a muscular man. Then, coming from the right, in the periphery of my vision, I see a bhikkhuni, whose soft hairless face peers into mine.

"Venerable Sujata, I feared the worst," Padmapani says with true feeling in her voice. Being conscious of her compassion brings me fully awake faster than someone pouring water on my face.

"Like I said, he is all right," a disconcerted male voice says, and then I recognize it, not by the sound, but by associating it with Padmapani, as Kunika speaking.

"Kunika is right," I say. "I am fine. I just needed a nap and forgot it was nearing time for your lesson."

"We need not have it today if you are not well," she says.

"If we postpone your lesson every time I nap during the day, or feel a little weak, then you will certainly have no more lessons from me." I attempt to chuckle and look cheerful as I round off this sentence, but that does not wipe the concern off her face, though it brings a smile to Kunika, who no doubt sees me as a silly old man.

Kunika drops the smile and says, "Can you not see, Sister, that this elder is losing his faculties, and it will not be long before you must find another teacher?"

"But first," she says with strength, determination, and dare I say, love, in her voice, "before his faculties decline, I will learn all I can from him."

I am touched by her attachment to me and awed by her determination to learn as much as she can from me. This is the highest form of devotion I have ever received from a student. Now, I am eager to instruct.

But my memory fails me, so I ask, "What is today's lesson?"

"We were to begin the eightfold path," Padmapani says.

"Then tell me," I ask, "what is the eightfold path?"

"It is the middle way."

"What is the middle way?"

She says, "It is the way that lies between the extremes of self-indulgence and self-mortification."

"So it is neither self-indulgence nor self-mortification? Or is it just a little of each, where they meet in the middle?" I ask, delighted with my use of logic.

Kunika interrupts before Padmapani has a chance to answer. I would not mind him doing this so much if he were truly interested, but he seems to interject his questions as a way to confuse me. As an old man, once diverted, it is hard to find my way back to where I left off.

Kunika says, "That is very clever. The middle way is thus either the way of moderation, for that is what a little self-indulgence and a little self-mortification add up to, or it is a way that does not include either of them, which would be what?"

Padmapani then says, "The arising of the vision through which the Dhamma becomes known."

"What does that mean?" Kunika says.

"She is right," I say.

"Then explain it to me in clear, precise terms," Kunika says.

Padmapani says, "From seeing the Dhamma, one understands the middle way. The middle way is the way of no more doubt about the teaching. It comes about from the arising of the eye of knowledge, which dispels ignorance."

Kunika, his irritation obviously growing, says, "Can you be any more abstruse? Is there a simpler way of saying the same thing?"

Padmapani replies, "The meaning of the Buddha's discourses are clear to those who hear them repeatedly, but not so to those who have not studied them."

"Then someone needs to put these teachings into an orderly form," Kunika says.

I say, "You are speaking of the Abhidhamma."

"This is the first time I have heard of it," Kunika says. "What is the Abhidhamma?"

"The Abhidhamma extracts from the Buddha's discourses what is taught repeatedly, thereby stripping the teaching of all ambiguity and metaphor. What is left is the pure essence of the Buddha's Dhamma."

"That is exactly what I would like to know," Kunika says, his face beaming at this discovery. "Is there a bhikkhu in Kusinara who teaches the Abhidhamma?"

"No. You must travel to one of big centers of learning. You may find such teachers in Vesali, Savatthi, or Rajagaha."

Then, turning to Padmapani, Kunika asks, "Does such a journey appeal to you?"

Padmapani's face reddens and tears up. She says, "I cannot leave Venerable Sujata. What would happen to him? Besides, I am not drawn to the Abhidhamma. I love the stories, the metaphors, and the simplicity of the Buddha's words. That is why I have chosen Venerable Sujata as my teacher."

"Very well," he says. "Then I will go on my own and you will have to find someone else to sit with you during these lessons."

"Very well," she says, wiping a tear from her eye, smiling at me briefly before getting up to leave. "Then I shall see you tomorrow, Venerable Sujata."

"Yes," I say, my heart aching for her to stay. Perhaps, my mind can conjure up her soothing presence when she leaves, and I may rest sweetly for the remainder of my days. It is such fantasies that feed the kamma of my next birth. If I were not a bhikkhu, I would say, "Let *Metta* be my Master."

V

The days to the next uposatha pass with a single purpose in mind. Kunika continues to accompany Padmapani for her daily lessons, though he does announce that he plans to leave for Vesali on the day of the full moon, which coincides with the uposatha. We must find someone to replace him by that time because I will need Padmapani's help to get myself ready to recite the fortnightly *Patimokkha* to the assembly of bhikkhus.

We find a samanera this time. His name is Kassapa, a worthy name, which reminds me of the arahant, Mahakassapa.

Mahakassapa was on his way to Kusinara when he heard that the Buddha had passed into parinibbana but a few days before. He quickened his pace and arrived in Kusinara after the Malla chiefs had tried to burn the Buddha's body but could not. It was rumored that the gods would not allow the Buddha's body to be burned. But when Mahakassapa arrived at the Buddha's funeral pyre, he bowed to the Buddha and then walked three times around the Buddha's corpse. When he finished, he lifted the cloth to expose the Buddha's feet. Mahakassapa touched his head to the Buddha's toes. Several of the bhikkhus did the same. The funeral pyre was then lit. The flames climbed high into the heavens.

This new Kassapa is a perfect samanera. He is quiet, respectful, intelligent, and kind. He accompanied Padmapani for her lesson yesterday and sat attentively as we discussed the merits of the middle way. Today, she must come early for her lesson, as it is the uposatha. She needs time to wash my robe and sweep around my hut, while Kassapa can shave my head and beard. Then there is the matter of cleaning my hut. It will be faster if Kassapa can help her with that as well. Kunika would never help her. He would just sit and watch, thinking to himself, and it would have been improper for me to ask him to do anything for me. But a samanera like Kassapa, who must be no more than fifteen years old, will feel compelled to help an elderly bhikkhu, and will most certainly ask me if there is anything I need.

I do not know how much time I have until they arrive. All I know is that I have already eaten today. I will just have to sit here and wait for them.

Being alone with my thoughts has never been pleasant. I guess that is why I never meditated. Whenever I was alone, I would recite some verses to purportedly memorize the Dhamma, but I have come to realize that I used the Buddha's words mostly to replace my ordinary thoughts with his enlightened ideas. Because I am not going over the Buddha's words in my mind anymore, I have more stray thoughts, more unwholesome thoughts. The only thing that works to keep my mind off these unwanted thoughts is the contemplation of death. Though sometimes the thought of death brings up unwholesome thoughts about what I missed by being a bhikkhu for my whole adult life. So, when contemplating death does not work, I think about full liberation of mind and wonder if I have an inkling of what that is. For if I had such knowledge, then, maybe, I may be reborn as a god. But I always conclude that I am still ignorant. Why is liberating knowledge so hard to come by?

Thinking about the Dhamma like this always goes in circles. Perhaps my major doubt, the big unanswered question, is what happens when we die. The Buddha enters parinibbana while other beings go on to a new life, not knowing beforehand what that life will be. I can grasp the idea of going on to a new life, but I cannot fathom what parinibbana is. I was at the Buddha's parinibbana, yet that seems to make it more of a mystery. There are many people, bhikkhus mostly, who seem to have no problem believing that the Buddha entered parinibbana, and they were not there.

The idea of parinibbana is not so simple. It only occurs upon the physical death of an arahant. It is widely believed that arahants go beyond existence and enter into a permanent, empty, stable state, where there is no coming and going, no elements, no being, just the final resting place. No one lives there and no one returns from there. It is the end of existence. Yet it is also peaceful and supremely happy.

Renewed existence is something I can understand. My fears, desires, ambitions, and sorrows do not evaporate upon my death, but propel me into a new life where I find nourishment for the same fears and new ones, building new desires upon old ones, creating so much activity, doing so much work to stay alive and make this new life into something that I become swallowed up by it and think of it as mine forever. Then I perish again and am reborn in a lower realm, doing what needs to be done to ensure my survival, so that if I am a lion, I kill and eat what I kill, thus producing a next life and several thereafter in lower realms of fear, pain, and ignorance. The downward spiral through the animal realms to the realms of torment seems so real to me that I must have slipped and tumbled through them countless times.

Rebirth in the human realm would therefore be a blessing, one I should not dismiss just yet. I so wanted to be born among the gods. After several hours of memorizing the Buddha's words, I would daydream about being born into one of the heavenly realms, weighing each one by the kinds of delights I would enjoy, conjuring up those pleasures so vividly I could see, hear, and touch them. The higher material and immaterial realms of existence did not attract me, for they seemed so sterile, so dull, and were by their very nature out of my reach. But the lesser material realms, where there were a variety of pleasures, including that of being loved by beautiful goddesses, drew me into the sweetest daytime reveries. I yearn to be born as a god, to live thousands of years in a realm of bliss and love, where I can forget about the horrors and sorrows of existence and the noble search for that which is beyond existence. I just want to experience celestial happiness when I die. Nothing more. Have I not done enough, put myself through enough deprivation, followed the rules and their intent, to deserve such a birth?

I wish I did not have to wait to die to find out. The Buddha was fortunate to be certain about his destination after death. I wish he were here to tell me mine.

VI

Young Kassapa and Padmapani arrive. They help me up, as I am feeling unusually weak. I lean against them as they lead me outside to a stump of wood. I sit down slowly, for I fear falling over.

It takes me a while to catch my breath. Kassapa looks up into my eyes from where he kneels on the hard earth, and I see a blend of wisdom and compassion in his eyes. He can become the arahant I could not. Let me impart some of the Dhamma to him before I depart. That gift alone can win me a place in the realm of the gods.

Padmapani returns with a basin of water and a knife. It is time for Kassapa to shave my head, but I do not want him to. I want to teach the Dhamma.

"Padmapani," I say, somewhat surprised that I am still out of breath, "let us wait to have Kassapa shave my head. Right now, I would like to impart the essence of the Dhamma."

She sits down, with the bowl in her lap and the knife in her right hand, and I think of her name referring to her holding a lotus in one hand. My imagination conjures up a white lotus that opens to reveal, in its center, a gleaming knife. I jolt upright. Padmapani jumps, spilling the bowl of water, dropping the knife on the ground as she rushes to my side.

"Not yet, I am still alive."

She looks relieved and sits down near my feet as Kassapa picks up the knife and sets the bowl upright on the ground.

"I can still teach. Now listen closely."

I clear my throat, coughing a couple of times, which alarms her but not Kassapa, who sits with his arms crossed, his gaze fixed on me.

"Why is it that the truth of existence can be best known in a human birth? It is because we are conceived in a womb, concealed in darkest ignorance for nine months, and when we are born, the chances of our dying and our mother's dying are great. If we pass into this world without losing our own or our mother's life, or being crippled and sickly from birth, we have but sidestepped enormous suffering for just a little while. In our youth we can starve, fall deathly ill to the elements, have injuries inflicted on us by others, or be abandoned by our parents. If that does not happen, we have but sidestepped enormous suffering for just a little while. By the age of six years old, we can begin to learn from life and know the truth of our existence as suffering. From then on, suffering and the knowledge of suffering can walk together, and one need not suffer ignorantly. But that is not possible for most human beings, since they lack the wisdom to learn from their misfortunes and sorrows.

"The gods are not born with such precariousness, nor do they have the conditions in their world to create the depth and variety of pain and torment that we have in the human realm. They begin happy and would only know the pain of their existence when a loved one perishes. That is why the Buddha taught that the gods cannot find liberation for themselves and must be taught the path to liberation. We, on the other hand, can find liberation for ourselves, for we can experience the truth of existence: Life is painful from the beginning, in the middle, and at the end."

Padmapani's face shines with love. Then I fall to the ground.

When I return to consciousness, I feel my head resting in Padmapani's lap. I cannot see anything, but I can hear two voices, his and hers, talking loudly.

"Run! Get help!" Padmapani says.

"But I cannot leave you alone with a bhikkhu," Kassapa says.

"Forget those rules! He is dying!"

"You are right!"

"Go! Get help!"

Kassapa kicks some dirt on my face as he runs off.

Her lotus soft hands wipe away the dirt and then soothe my face.

I feel loved and so feel love back.

Then I...

Myth
of
Maitreya

Jason Siff

Vasubandhu's Commentary on the Life of Maitreya

PROLOGUE

Writing a biography should be no different from writing a commentary to a sacred text. I have written several commentaries in my long life, but never a biography. My method of writing scriptural commentary is to first present a verse to be analyzed, and, only then, insert an explanation that elucidates its hidden meaning. Were it not for my commentaries, many scriptures, especially those ascribed to Maitreya, would be incomprehensible and essentially worthless for aspiring bodhisattvas.

My biography of Maitreya should be set down in a similar way. The story of the next Buddha must not be told resorting to the detestable practice of myth-making, so common among modern-day Buddhists, though I cannot prevent the damage already done by my elder brother, Asanga, who at least had the privilege of meeting Maitreya, while I have not. I begrudgingly trust Asanga's motives for creating a mythic Maitreya, for without his outlandish story, there probably would not be any serious public interest in Maitreya's teachings (outside of my brilliant commentaries).

To set the record straight, I shall begin with the illusions germinated and spread by Asanga's fantastic imagination, stating them blatantly in a manner which dispels them at the same time. Asanga proclaimed to the world that Maitreya visited him, of all the *bhikshus* in India, because he was determined to find the liberation of mind known only by the Buddhas and was not satisfied with the Arhat Path (as I was at that time). Asanga had gone to the forest to meditate and after twelve years arrived at nothing. Then one day, he found a mangy dog with maggots crawling on its flesh. He used his mouth to gently capture the maggots clinging to the dog's wounds so as not to kill a single being, no matter how insignificant, and then tended to the wounded dog until it recovered. Only then did the dog reveal its true identity as Maitreya, appearing only to Asanga's eyes, for no one else could see the bodhisattva. From that day on, Maitreya spoke to Asanga, who memorized and preserved what he heard for posterity.

Not long after Asanga's return to the world, I first heard the teachings of Maitreya. Once I determined the importance of these teachings, I pressed my brother to introduce me to this original thinker. He refused, telling me the story I have just related. He added that no one can ever see Maitreya since, he stated cryptically, Maitreya cannot be found in any realm of existence. My brother's behavior led me to believe that he fabricated the whole incident, and that he was the real author of Maitreya's poems. But after an exhaustive examination of Maitreya's verses while composing my commentaries on them, I reached the conclusion that Asanga could not have created them. They were fashioned by someone far more intelligent than Asanga. I could have written them. But I didn't.

Years later, after my brother had composed many treatises based on Maitreya's teachings and I had completed my brilliant commentaries, Asanga confided in me the real story of the person known as Maitreya. This conversation took place a few months before his passing and lasted several hours. What follows should be an accurate recounting of this strange and suspicious story, even though many years have passed since I heard it.

I

Asanga's claim to have gone to the forest to meditate for twelve years is entirely trustworthy. There was a thirteen-year period of my life when I did not see my brother, and no one knew where he was. At the time, I held the opinion that Asanga had gone to a far-off land, never to return. Toward the end of this period, I heard a rumor that he was staying at a monastery in nearby Taxila. I decided to go there myself, only to discover that Asanga's fame was being used to attract visitors to this monastery in need of help.

As it turned out, Asanga was staying in the foothills of Nepal, living under an assumed name. He lived in a small mud hut with a thatched roof on the outskirts of a tiny village. He had no visitors for a long time, since no one knew who he was, or so he thought. Then one day, after going undetected for nearly twelve years, an old bhikshu appeared outside his hut.

The bhikshu said, "I have heard that a great teacher lives here."

"I am a teacher, but not a great one."

"That is for time to tell. Are you not Asanga?"

Asanga was astonished at hearing his name. He had misgivings about revealing his identity, but something spoke to him, perhaps his conscience saying, *You must not break the precept on lying.*

"Yes, you have found me. I am Asanga."

The bhikshu smiled, void of teeth, at Asanga's confession.

He said, "There is no need to be ashamed for having misled people as to your real name. Your intentions are noble, and, to your mind, necessary. But one who seeks the Truth must also tell the truth.

"You may not believe what I am about to reveal. But know I have never lied in my sixty years as a bhikshu. I have an important message for you. The Bodhisattva Maitreya wishes to make known his teaching and has chosen you to be his chronicler."

"How can that be?" Asanga said, even more astonished than before. His wish had come true. These twelve years would not be fruitless after all. Instantly trusting the old bhikshu, he was eager to begin.

"What must I do?"

The old bhikshu said, "Each night, leave the window nearest your bed open. Lie down in your bed and wait. Maitreya will then come to you. But remember, do not get up from the bed or speak to the bodhisattva. Your task is to commit the bodhisattva's words to memory. That is all."

"How will I know if it is indeed Maitreya who is speaking to me?" Asanga said, realizing that he was not going to see the bodhisattva if he did as the old bhikshu instructed.

The bhikshu said, "Once you have heard the teaching of Maitreya, you may then decide if it is truly the Buddha's teaching. But, you must give it time to make sense."

And then, as mysteriously as the old bhikshu appeared, he vanished. Asanga sat in meditation, determined to purify his mind as a way to know for certain the difference between what is real and what is an illusion appearing to be real. Only with a luminous, clear mind would he be able to tell if what he heard was truly the Buddha's teaching and not a counterfeit teaching. The Buddha's prophecy obsessed him at that time, for it was commonly believed that the Dharma would disappear after five hundred years. Only after the Dharma had been lost for some time would Maitreya appear in the world. This prospect excited my brother to no end and may have served to make him more gullible than usual, except for his suspicion. There was another tradition, which my brother was also familiar with, that stated when the Buddha's Dharma vanished from the world, a counterfeit Dharma would replace it. That thought scared Asanga, for he did not want to be the chronicler of the counterfeit Dharma.

After the sun had set, Asanga decided to lie down on his bed, with the window wide open, expecting to stay awake all night to no avail. The first few hours passed without the bodhisattva making an appearance. Normally, Asanga would fall asleep toward midnight and wake again before dawn. But as midnight approached, he used many tricks to keep himself awake. He pinched himself repeatedly, kept his eyes open with both thumbs and index fingers, and even resorted to fanciful daydreams meant to excite his mind. Still, he fell asleep sometime after midnight.

Asanga dreamed of returning from alms round and coming across a dog lying in the middle of the path. He could not step around it. The dog looked up at him and he looked down at it, noticing that it had insects crawling around its body and head. He knelt down and began to lick the insects off the dog. When they were all gone, safely deposited away from the path in the bushes, he smiled down at the dog, pleased with how he saved the poor animal's life. Just then, the dog's eyes turned into human eyes, and the dog's body stretched and transformed into a reclining Buddha.

The Buddha began to speak to him in the dream, but Asanga could not remember a word, for he was awoken by a sweet soft voice blown on the breeze from the open window near his bed. This voice was reciting a poem. *This must be the visitation. The dream was an illusion! Or was it?*

He sat up in bed and strained his ear to hear each word, to absorb each verse, lodging them in his memory without criticism or analysis. He could examine the teachings within this poem after Maitreya had finished the recitation, which ended when the early morning sounds of the birds competed for his attention, eventually drowning out the bodhisattva's gentle voice.

When Asanga was certain that Maitreya had left, he rose from his bed and reviewed the verses he had memorized. He recounted them one at a time. It was after this initial review that he reached the conclusion that these were indeed the teachings of a Buddha. I would have needed several days to subject such teachings to counter-arguments before arriving at such a conclusion, but my brother Asanga was driven more by faith, less by reason, and so trusted his good fortune at having found Maitreya.

Asanga was so lost in concentration, reciting what he had heard throughout the day that he forgot to go on alms round and did not take an afternoon nap. By nightfall, he was extremely tired and so slipped into a deep sleep well before midnight. He slept longer than intended and woke up in the middle of a poem. He wished he could ask Maitreya to begin again. Then he remembered that he must not speak to Maitreya. Anyhow, how would he address the Buddha? It would not be possible to ask the bodhisattva to start over. He would just have to focus on what he heard and hope that one of these nights Maitreya would repeat the verses he missed.

That day, Asanga walked to the neighboring village for alms. A brahmin, who was also a prosperous farmer, invited him to accept alms indoors. Asanga was led to the largest room in the house. To his amazement, he saw the old toothless bhikshu seated on a bench, eating from his alms bowl. Asanga sat down on the bench next to him. The brahmin's two sons and wife came in and served freshly prepared food into his bowl. Asanga ate slowly, occasionally glancing over at the bhikshu.

When the bhikshu finished, he got up to empty his bowl and wash his hands. Asanga stopped eating and got up to follow him. The bhikshu walked into the courtyard and emptied the remainders into a hole in the ground. Asanga watched him and then did the same. He then scooped some water out of a wooden trough and washed his hands and face. Asanga moved next to him and did the same. The bhikshu looked over at Asanga and smiled with his bare gums.

"You seem convinced that the verses you hear in the middle of the night, when you could be sleeping, belong to Maitreya," he said.

"It was wrong for me to doubt you," Asanga said, "even for a moment."

"But you have one misgiving."

"Yes," Asanga said, wondering if his facial expressions are that easy to read. "I missed the first half of last night's poem. Will Maitreya repeat those verses for me?"

"That is something we have no control over. Recite all that you have memorized. In Maitreya's omniscience, the bodhisattva will know exactly what you have missed or forgotten."

"If Maitreya is omniscient, then he can hear this conversation and knows that I did not hear the first part of last night's poem."

The old bhikshu chuckled.

"Why would Maitreya bother to listen in on a conversation between two bhikshus? The bodhisattvas have adoration for the Dharma being recited and listen to nothing else. Recite the pure and true teachings! Only then will Maitreya know what it is you also need to know."

Asanga returned to his hut and sat in meditation. Not long after closing his eyes, he saw an image of Gautama Buddha reclining on his right side as he did at his parinirvana. Asanga imagined that now was his time to receive the Buddha's final teaching.

From the moment of my enlightenment to this moment before my passing, I have not proclaimed a doctrine.

Asanga already knew this verse from the *Lankavatara Sutra*. What it meant to him at that moment most interests me here. Gautama Buddha taught an incomplete Dharma. In other words, Maitreya is the Buddha who teaches the perfected Dharma, the way of the bodhisattva, while Gautama Buddha taught only the inferior way of the arhat. This truly is the new Dharma that Asanga had gone to the forest to discover!

And so, with a fervor supporting an inexhaustible wakefulness, Asanga listened nightly to the teachings of Maitreya, chronicling them for posterity.

II

Being a Buddhist scholar with a reputation to keep, I feel it is my duty to explain Asanga's use of the term, "bodhisattva." He uses the word as though he invented it. Granted, he did reinvent it, and it is that interpretation which needs further explanation in light of what preceded it.

It is here that my skills as an expounder and annotator of texts are most helpful. I hope to clear up some of the confusion my brother has generated on this important subject. Asanga was captivated by the tales of bodhisattvas and the spiritual feats they accomplished. I believe his exuberance blinded him to some of the obvious contradictions surrounding bodhisattvas and their place in the scheme of things.

Now the term "bodhisattva" comes from combining two words: *bodhi*, meaning wise or awakened, and *sattva*, a being. Those two words combined should mean, "an awakened being." But that would make the terms "Buddha" and "bodhisattva" indistinguishable. That is why I must then go back to how these two designations are used in the *Tripitaka*. There one finds that the Buddha is a "fully awakened individual," while a bodhisattva is "someone who is destined to become a Buddha."

The Tripitaka tradition states that there is only one way to become a bodhisattva. The bodhisattva must be a bhikshu who takes a vow to become a future Buddha in the presence of the current Buddha. This bhikshu must be an exceptional being to do so. He could, if he so pleased, realize nirvana were he not to take the vow. There was only one bhikshu we know of who took the bodhisattva vow from Gautama Buddha, and that was a bhikshu by the name of Maitreya. It is this same Maitreya who is supposed to appear once Gautama Buddha's teaching has disappeared and the counterfeit teachings have emerged in its place.

Soon after Gautama Buddha, new discourses, ones not found in the Tripitaka, began to appear. These discourses are believed to have come from the Buddha and are considered authentic teachings in the various sects that make up the Mahayana. These new teachings tend to portray the bodhisattva differently, setting the foundation for Asanga's reinterpretation.

A bodhisattva is no longer required to make his vow before a Buddha. Another bodhisattva will do. Though that creates a quandary in my mind. Who was the first bodhisattva to do this? The answer lies in the belief that there are many more bodhisattvas than Maitreya, some of whom periodically take human form. Now, according to an authoritative treatise on the subject, a bodhisattva can only incarnate as a male and must ordain as a bhikshu when he is of an age to do so. Asanga believed that there are bodhisattvas alive now, living as ordinary bhikshus. He believed he was one of them. In fact, he was the only bodhisattva, to my knowledge, who had taken the vow from Maitreya Buddha, making him a true bodhisattva in the original sense.

Now back to the topic of this section. Asanga reinvented the idea of a bodhisattva in the creation of special teachings meant only for bodhisattvas. There needed to be particular practices and higher realizations that distinguished a bodhisattva from an ordinary bhikshu with his 227 rules, fortnightly *Pratimoksha*, and *smrty-upasthana* meditations. The bodhisattva had to have a path nobler than the eightfold path, for his calling was to be a future Buddha, not a mere disciple. And it is here that Asanga began to think in terms of higher levels of realization and tremendous acts of selflessness, for the bodhisattva had to become a superhuman spiritual hero destined to deliver beings to nirvana on a grander scale than ever before imaginable.

And, for Asanga, all this rested on the authority that he was chosen to chronicle Maitreya's Dharma and bring those teachings into the world.

III

Weeks went by where Asanga was visited nightly by the sweet, gentle voice that delighted his ears with Maitreya's teachings. After the last recitation, Maitreya said, "Now take these teachings to those who aspire to fulfill the middle way, for they are in need of the true Mahayana."

Asanga was saddened by this abrupt ending, even though he knew it was coming, for how many times would Maitreya repeat the same teachings? As excited as he was to bring these teachings to the Sangha, he feared the realistic prospect of encountering resistance to these new ideas. He did not know where to go to find a sympathetic audience and was reminded of Gautama Buddha, who, when he agreed to teach the Dharma, lamented that there was too much dust in the eyes of too many. It was in this regard that the old bhikshu was most helpful.

"It is well known that you, Asanga, went to the forest to find the teaching of the Buddhas. The bhikshus belonging to your monastery certainly anticipate your return, eager to hear the Dharma you have mastered in your solitude."

Asanga agreed with the old bhikshu and intended to take his advice. But, a peculiar form of doubt gnawed at him. It was not doubt in Maitreya's teachings, for he had examined them thoroughly enough, for his temperament, to find them convincing. He reasoned that because he had not really seen Maitreya, how did he know that it was really Maitreya who spoke to him? This is somewhat illogical, since it is what the Buddha says, not what he looks like, that gives validity to his teaching. And if what was said was Buddha-like, then why the need to have seen the Buddha? But here Asanga was far more astute than I would have been in a similar situation. He knew that no matter how profound and exceptional Maitreya's teachings were, no one would believe they belonged to the next Buddha unless he could say that he had seen Maitreya with his own eyes. So, he wove together a story based on his dream of seeing the mangy dog transform into the Buddha. He went over his fanciful story several times until he believed it himself, thereby turning it into a credible and real myth. Only then was he ready to return to his home monastery.

Asanga arrived at his home monastery in a couple of weeks, addressing an assembly of bhikshus the night following his arrival. His discourse began by introducing Maitreya's teaching simply as a teaching of the Bodhisattva Path. He neglected to mention the story of meeting Maitreya, perhaps sensing that this was not the right time to do so. Instead, he related the central philosophy of Maitreya's teaching.

The monks listened to Asanga speak on the nature of emptiness, and those steeped in the philosophy of the emptiness of all things were pleased at how similar this new teaching was to their own. Once Asanga felt assured that his listeners agreed with his ideas, he went into the three essences of the new teaching. He spoke of the primary essence of *Interdependency* and touched on the interplay between the *Grasper* and the *Grasped*. The second essence, known as the *Imagination of the Unreal*, he described in terms that associated it with the illusory nature of all things in the minds of his listeners. The third and final essence was most difficult to explain, so he left it as broad as he could, saying that it was the *Accomplished,* the *Perfected,* and the *Highest Realization.*

Asanga's discourse would have gone well had he left off philosophizing at this point. But he could read the atmosphere in the room, which was hungry for the Dharma, very hungry indeed, and so he set out on another course. He brought up what he referred to as the *Abhidharma* of this new teaching, which was not like any Abhidharma I have ever studied, and I am an expert on the Abhidharma. He told his audience that it was a new perspective on the nature of consciousness. Many of the bhikshus squirmed uncomfortably at this notion, for they were satisfied with the traditional well-proven theories of consciousness and were not inclined to hear another. Asanga should have recognized the signs of discomfort in his audience, but he was so enthralled by what he was about to say that he plunged ahead.

I wish I had been at his side when he began talking about Consciousness-Only, as I surely would have persuaded him to be silent on the subject. Asanga presented the idea that there are two types of consciousness, one experiential, and the other, a transcendent consciousness that contained all karmic seeds. What his fellow bhikshus heard was not the Buddha's teaching, but Vedanta of the most heretical sort. Asanga was accused of asserting the doctrine of an eternal Self. The bhikshus left furious. Asanga was humiliated. Because of that, Maitreya's philosophy also became known as, "The Doctrine of Consciousness-Only."

Asanga was so shaken by the antipathy he felt from his fellow bhikshus that he left the monastery immediately afterward. He walked to another town where he found a room in a small monastery to sleep for the night. He barely slept at all and left before dawn, not knowing his next destination. While walking alone on the road, he saw a *sadhu* meditating under a tree. He approached the tree and sat down facing the sadhu. He was exhausted and his mind could not hold onto any subject of concentration. His thoughts kept returning to his failure and humiliation at presenting Maitreya's ideas. He defended himself in his mind, feeling unjustly accused of heresy. Then, out of the blue, the mendicant spoke.

"Truth is muddied by the mind. Consciousness-Only knows what is true, without concepts."

Asanga contemplated this statement for a few moments. This was consistent with Maitreya's teaching, boosting Asanga's mood in anticipation for what the sadhu might say next.

As Asanga waited for the next message, his mind grew sleepy and he began to relive in a dream the events of the day before. But this time, the sadhu was in the hall with all the bhikshus, dressed only in a loin cloth, his skin mud-caked and foul, standing with a Shiva trident in his right hand. He was blind, looking directly at Asanga through empty sockets. His lips moved in slow motion, uttering these words:

"Realization, learning, and what one calls truth are all constructions of the imagination. Container Consciousness is neither self nor no-self. It transcends the two extremes."

I could not have said it better and am grateful to this sadhu, whoever, or whatever, he was, for appearing in Asanga's dream at this time. For this dream became the catalyst for Asanga's new crusade, where I played a crucial role.

IV

A biography is about history, and I have given you very little of my own history, particularly as it pertains to my brother Asanga and the mysterious Maitreya. Being a person who is often talked about by others, I also have myths surrounding my life that need to be dispelled, and what better place to do so than here. So, what follows is a short commentary on my life as it relates to both Asanga and Maitreya.

Asanga was nearly twenty years older than me. Our father was a brahmin priest, learned in the Vedas. He was not pleased by Asanga's decision to join the Sangha in his twentieth year. When Asanga would visit us, our father would not bow to him to show respect. Instead, he would wait for Asanga to bow to him first. They would stand looking at each other, neither of them showing the other the expected form of respect, until Asanga would politely request to speak to my mother alone. Our father would then leave without saying a word.

My brother impressed me. As a small boy I aspired to be like him. Asanga was a paragon of gentleness. I never heard my brother raise his voice or argue with another. He was extremely patient, as his relationship with our father surely attests, and to my young mind he seemed to be more like a god than a man. But he would not speak to me of his spiritual path, saying that I was too young to concern myself with esoteric matters.

During my school years, Asanga's visits became less frequent, and when I was eight years old, he disappeared from my life altogether. This was the twelve-year period of his seclusion in the forest, but I did not know that then, for no one in my family knew Asanga's true intentions. Our father was convinced that his eldest son had left the world and would never return, and my mother (Asanga's mother had died after he was born and our father married her younger sister) worried about Asanga constantly, for she had raised him and loved him as much as her own son. When I was twelve years old, I vowed to search for Asanga, primarily to relieve my mother's distress, but also to prove my father wrong.

Then I got sidetracked. In my fifteenth year, I began studying the Abhidharma. I enrolled in a local school dedicated to the Abhidharma teachings of the *Vaibhasika's*. I was a zealous student. Most of all, I enjoyed debating with my teachers. I earned the reputation as the foremost debater in all of Purushapura, which was an incredible feat for a young man who was still not old enough to become a bhikshu.

In the meantime, I decided to learn all I could about the Abhidharma. From my home in Gandhara, I walked to Kashmir, where I was told the most knowledgeable Abhidharma scholars of our age lived. But these Kashmiri scholars looked down on us outsiders. They went so far as to instruct their king to make sure that such inferior students of the Abhidharma were turned back at the border. That is why I dressed in rags and acted like a madman. The border guards just laughed at my antics and let me pass into their country.

The study of the Abhidharma is a very serious occupation. The Kashmiri scholars were the most serious-minded men I have ever met, so it was quite easy for me to fool them into believing I was a lunatic. All I had to do was say something unrelated every second sentence, augmenting my logical discourse with mad and irrelevant outbursts. In this manner, I was able to live in their presence and listen to their teachings without one of them realizing that I could steal these teachings and do whatever I wanted with them. I wish I could have seen the look on their faces when they read my dictionary of the Abhidharma. One of these scholars sent me a bag of gold coins to write a commentary to my dictionary, but I returned it, for I had gotten what I wanted from them and did not want to be bound by their patronage.

I stayed at a monastery in town and began to teach what I had learned in Kashmir. Each day, I would compose a philosophical proposition based on the Abhidharma, which I would then engrave on a copper plate. I would attach a rope to the piece of copper and drape it around an elephant's neck. Then I would lead the elephant through town, challenging people to refute my statement of the day.

As I taught the more rigid and complex Abhidharma of the Kashmiri scholars, I soon began to examine their ideas. After thoroughly examining the flaws in their formulations, I decided to study a less complicated Abhidharma, called *Sautrantika*, which was believed to have come directly from the Buddha. I found the simplicity and clarity of the Sautrantika teachings refreshing, but still not altogether satisfying.

The Abhidharma is a descriptive system delineating how consciousness functions. It categorizes states of consciousness, analyzes them, and states rules of combination and exclusion. At its heart is the belief that only the present moment exists, and thus consciousness, like everything else, is constantly arising and passing away. There is no connection between one moment and the next. Each moment of consciousness is unique and will never be experienced again. Consciousness is real. There is no illusion about it, though it can contain delusion.

I encountered the Mahayana teachings on emptiness after having studied the Abhidharma, so I was not accustomed to seeing things as empty. I had been debating for years on the premise that all mental phenomena were substantial and complete. I could talk about a mind-state of desire as though it were a tree, the earth, or the sun, and describe the laws of desire just as an astrologer can chart and predict the movements of celestial bodies.

For many years, I had eagerly attacked the idea that desire is insubstantial and empty, defeating proponents of that view in debate, never once giving it a second thought. Then what happened to me? This is an important part for my inclusion in this story, for if I had continued as a teacher of the Abhidharma, I would never have been interested in the new teachings of Maitreya. What happened was that I read some of the most advanced formulations of the Mahayana teachings on the emptiness of all things and began to think deeply about that possibility. What if desire was like a soap bubble? Solid on the outside, empty on the inside. And, if I expanded that to include all mental and physical phenomena, what did that say about the world we inhabit? On the surface, all is in flux, as in the Abhidharma, but underneath, all is empty. The world rests on nothing, but that is an illusion too. Emptiness is not nothingness. Then what is emptiness? Is it nirvana?

I know the answers now, but back then I kept asking myself these questions and consulted as many Mahayana teachings as I could. There were weeks of sleepless nights when it cost me a considerable sum to keep the oil lamps burning. And, it was at that time I thought again of Asanga and so sought him out. As I mentioned earlier, I did not find Asanga then. It was a year later.

V

After Asanga's failure to bring Maitreya's teaching to the bhikshus at his home monastery, he went from one monastery to another for several weeks, finally settling at the deer park in Sarnath. He found the place where Gautama Buddha gave his first discourse to be restful and inspiring. On the day I arrived, I found him meditating under a large pipal tree. I sat down next to him and closed my eyes. As I breathed in, I felt excitement at being with my elder brother at last, and as breathed out, I hoped that we would be together for a long time.

Asanga opened his eyes first. He did not recognize me, since the last time he saw me I was only eight years old. When I opened my eyes and saw him looking at me, I introduced myself. To my surprise, he embraced me. In that moment, I experienced an expansive emotional mind-state, one that infused my life with enduring meaning.

We walked around the deer park. Asanga asked me about our parents. I told him what little I knew, for I had not seen much of them since becoming a bhikshu. He expressed a wish to see our parents before they died, but that would have to wait until he had finished this next phase of organizing the teachings of Maitreya.

Asanga then stated how auspicious it was that I had found him at that moment in time. He predicted that my skill in debate and my penchant for writing commentaries would be instrumental in enabling these teachings to withstand the scrutiny of scholars.

Now that I was included in Asanga's project for Maitreya's teachings, I became curious about the author of them. At first, I thought that Asanga was referring to a fellow bhikshu. Then, as Asanga said more about the author, it dawned on me that he was attributing these teachings to the bodhisattva who would become the next Buddha. That revelation rekindled my inexhaustible drive to find the true Dharma, when it should have aroused my suspicion, especially since Asanga then told me the story of the miraculous transformation of a maggot-infested dog into an embodied bodhisattva.

So, with the rapturous enthusiasm of an entranced devotee, I am ashamed to admit, I begged Asanga to recite some of Maitreya's teachings.

Asanga stopped below the monumental stupa at Sarnath, towering higher than two royal palaces stacked one upon the other, and spoke in a booming voice as if addressing an assembly of bhikshus instead of his only brother.

In the imagination
There is no duality,
But there is emptiness.
In emptiness,
There is imagination as well.

I was stunned by the profundity of these verses, but more so struck by how well they addressed my new way of thinking. I asked Asanga to repeat them, so that I could memorize them without error, but instead he continued:

Because of that,
Imagination is neither empty nor non-empty.
It creates, annihilates, and renews.
That is the middle way.

And there it was, the new teaching all spelled out for me. The middle way is to know the mind. Consciousness is, at its core, empty, but the imagination is neither empty nor non-empty. It is both the source of suffering and the path to end it, though the end of suffering is not to be found in the imagination. Nirvana is not what we imagine it to be. Neither empty nor non-empty, it is and it is not, and therefore it is.

Now, as I look back on this extraordinary life-changing realization, I can see that my infatuation with these new teachings was in part due to my love and admiration for Asanga. I could not see it then, but I am sure that when my brother spoke those verses beneath the towering stupa, I saw a Great Bodhisattva giving voice to the Dharma of the next Buddha.

I spent a year with Asanga in Sarnath, learning Maitreya's verses by heart. We worked day and night to present these new teachings in the clearest, most defensible form possible. Those were joyous times, working with my brother, and I have treasured them. If Asanga was not so eager to spread these teachings, I would have gladly spent several more years working together on the finer points.

Asanga lectured and wrote for thirty years, frequently
consulting the verses of Maitreya, winning over thousands of
adherents, forever changing the face of Mahayana Buddhism. His
writings are far more accessible to the novice than mine. And,
I give him credit for that. Though his writings did not change
much over this period, I could detect a shift in mood, a subtle
dampening of his enthusiasm midway through, and it was not
until he told me the rest of the story of Maitreya that I understood
the reason for it.

VI

More than a decade and a half later, Asanga found himself traveling through the general area where he lived in
solitude for all those years. He stopped at a monastery he had
not visited in the twelve years he was there, but had intended to,
for he had heard the villagers refer to this splendid monastery,
which claimed to have housed over fifty bhikshus, evenly divided
between Mahayana and Theravada, living in complete harmony.
But now the monastery only housed Mahayana bhikshus who
professed the new Dharma of Maitreya.

The bhikshus were so honored to have Asanga stay with
them, they gave him the best room and his own private servant
for the duration of his stay, which he extended from the intended
three days to five days. However, it was not the bhikshus generous
hospitality that led to Asanga's long stay, but rather something
he discovered on his third day there.

All the bhikshus in the monastery were invited to accept alms
at the house of a local merchant that day. Asanga initially declined
the invitation, as he was anxious to reach his next destination, but
was persuaded by the head monk of the monastery, who told him
that this merchant was eager to meet such a renowned teacher as
Asanga and would most certainly give a generous donation. My
brother was not one to pass up a substantial donation, especially
since there were monasteries, schools, hospitals, and orphanages
that relied on him.

Asanga was prepared to give a teaching on the middle way, if asked, and afterwards continue on his journey. He reached the merchant's estate just before noon, and so was required to eat as soon as everyone was seated. Though Asanga sat near the head of the group of bhikshus, no one present would have thought that he was any different from the other bhikshus. As he ate, he was relieved that he did have to speak to the assembly of laypeople gathered. After the meal, he could then quietly slip away after securing a generous donation.

When the meal was over and all the bhikshus had emptied their alms bowls, the head monk requested that they remain seated. Asanga was sure that he was going to be called upon to give the talk he had prepared for this occasion, but that was not the case. Instead, a senior nun, a *bhikshuni* with the unusual name of Buddhi, which is not quite the feminine form of Buddha, since it means "intellect" instead of "awakened," was brought out into the center of the room. She sat down on a cushion, crossing her legs and then positioning her hands in the teaching mudra. Her build was slim, of average height for a man, but tall for a woman, and her skin was light brown. Her features were pleasant but not beautiful, her shaved head was oval with a high forehead, and her face indicated her age to be over forty.

Asanga closed his eyes after making this extensive observation of the bhikshuni's appearance. As she spoke, he held her image in his mind. She chanted in a soft voice, oddly monotone, considering that most of Maitreya's teachings are chanted in a melodic fashion these days. What caught Asanga's attention was how this style of recitation, combined with the softness of her voice, reminded him of listening to Maitreya recite these very same verses over fifteen years ago. Only then did the connection between the two events erupt into Asanga's consciousness: *Buddhi was Maitreya!*

Asanga opened his eyes and stared at the bhikshuni as he concentrated on her chanting. He tried to notice the exact range of her voice, how she lengthened vowels, aspirated consonants, whether her pitch would rise at the end of a verse or remain constant. He concluded that her voice and Maitreya's were indeed identical. How did he not perceive this at the time? Of course, the voice that drifted into his room through the open window was a woman's voice. He briefly suspected it then, but told himself that a bodhisattva's voice would naturally be higher and sweeter than an ordinary man's. But now he was sure. His face reddened with anger at his foolishness. He had to do something about this deception. But what?

Over the next couple of days, Asanga kept to his room to figure out what he was going to do. Now that he knew it was a woman's voice, there were only two plausible explanations. One was that Maitreya spoke through this bhikshuni and the other was that this bhikshuni was the author of Maitreya's profound and stirring verses. If she was merely a human body Maitreya used to communicate with those in this realm of existence, then all was fine, but no longer ideal. But if Buddhi was the author, and therefore, there was no Maitreya, then Asanga had deceived the Sangha for sixteen years about the originator of the teachings he ardently professed.

But then Asanga assured himself that a woman could never create such verses. They exhibited a level of learning, intelligence, and artfulness that exceeded the genius of most men, so how could a woman accomplish it? It was then that Asanga imagined that the old bhikshu must have been the mastermind behind this spectacle. He taught his poems to this bhikshuni and had her recite them because Asanga would have recognized his voice. So, he decided to find the old bhikshu. He had to do that discreetly, for no one could suspect that Asanga, even for a moment, considered Maitreya was a hoax, because of all he had done to propagate these new teachings.

Asanga asked several bhikshus at the monastery if they knew of a toothless old bhikshu who traveled about in the villages where Asanga had stayed many years ago. One senior bhikshu remembered meeting this bhikshu, a true bodhisattva, who passed on some years ago. This information discouraged Asanga, though it did not stop him from inquiring further about the old bhikshu. The senior bhikshu told Asanga that he should visit a hermitage in a town not far from Asanga's old hut. He might find someone who knew the old bhikshu. Asanga's spirits lifted, and he set out on this journey the following morning.

Asanga arrived at the town before noon. Instead of stopping there for alms, he walked through the village to a road leading to a hermitage nestled in the hills. Halfway to the hermitage, Asanga met four bhikshus walking in the direction of the village. Asanga asked them to pause for a moment, so that he might ask them about the old toothless bhikshu, but they kept on walking. Asanga stood there baffled for a minute, not knowing what to do. Then he decided to follow the bhikshus back into the village, catching up with them just as they entered the town.

He tried to speak to them again, but they remained silent. Asanga wondered if they were practicing a vow of silence, but before he could broach the subject, the four bhikshus entered a courtyard where they were greeted by several men dressed in white. The bhikshus sat in a row on a rug. Asanga joined them, seating himself at the front of the row. No one asked him who he was. What Asanga recalled most was the heavy cast of silence. They were served in silence, ate in silence, emptied and cleaned their alms bowls in silence, and left without uttering a word.

When they arrived at their hermitage, Asanga was led to a room where he could take a nap. He asked again about the toothless bhikshu, but no one would speak to him. When he asked if they were observing a vow of silence, the bhikshus simply remained silent. Asanga had difficulty napping and so decided to get up and walk around the hermitage grounds to see if there was anyone else who might talk to him.

Giving up on the hermitage, Asanga went back to the village. On the outskirts, he saw a short obese bhikshu sweeping the ground in front of a tiny hut similar to the one he stayed in sixteen years ago. As he neared the hut, he got a better look this bhikshu and realized that she was a bhikshuni.

He interrupted her sweeping to ask her if she knew the toothless old bhikshu. The bhikshuni told Asanga to wait outside while she went into the hut. He could overhear her talking to somebody. Asanga had been harboring resentment from the quiet treatment he received from the bhikshus at the hermitage and was on the brink of letting his rage get the better of him. He had the impulse to barge into the little hut, but he pushed it aside in favor of patience. He began to generate compassion for himself as an antidote for the tide of anger surging within him. Finally, another bhikshuni emerged from the hut, her head bent demurely, offering her respects to Asanga, along with the customary request for compassion.

When she rose to stand opposite him, he immediately recognized her as the bhikshuni he heard reciting Maitreya's verses. Asanga could not believe his good fortune. He was so overjoyed at finding her that he had to check an impulse to embrace her.

"It is my good karma to have found you so easily! You are Buddhi? Am I correct?"

"Yes, I am Buddhi. Who are you?"

"I am Asanga," he said, looking into her eyes, trying to gauge what effect revealing his identity would have on her.

She appeared unimpressed.

"Your journey has been in vain," she said. "Dhira, the bhikshu you seek, entered Tushita Heaven several years ago."

"That does not change my purpose," Asanga said. "You may assist me in what I seek to know."

"I doubt that," she said.

"Can we sit somewhere and talk. Perhaps go inside?"

"That would not be proper," she said. "Our conduct would be questioned. We must remain in plain view."

"Forgive me. I often forget the rules for bhikshunis are stricter than they are for bhikshus. Is there a place we can sit and talk?"

Buddhi walked over to a log not far from the road and set a cloth on the ground in front of it. Asanga followed her and set his cloth on the log, sitting down on it. She sat cross-legged on the ground with her eyes closed in meditation while Asanga looked around him, wondering why she chose to meditate at that moment.

Asanga and the bhikshuni sat in silence for a long time. Villagers walked on the nearby road, glancing over at them, but none of them stopped. Asanga became acutely aware of the stench of oxen and cows. A breeze ruffled the hairs on his arms every couple of minutes, sending a chill across his shoulders. He would periodically open his eyes to peer at Buddhi to see if she had returned, for her face appeared to Asanga to be devoid of self, as if her mind had fled her body and wandered the skies above. Asanga was about to get up and leave when her face regained personality, which is more than just color and texture. He saw her eyes open with a sigh from having been refreshed and stilled within.

Buddhi said, "You would like to know more about Venerable Dhira. He was a perfect bhikshu and a true bodhisattva. What more do you need to know about him?"

"I met him once," Asanga said, "about sixteen years ago."

"You are that Asanga?" She exclaimed.

"Yes, I am. So, you know the story?"

"Not exactly."

"What do you know then?"

"I only know that you came here to live in solitude. You were seeking the teachings of Maitreya and Dhira brought them to you."

"And you were the one who recited Maitreya's verses. But those verses are not Maitreya's."

"What do you mean?"

"The old bhikshu, Dhira, he composed those verses."

Buddhi closed her eyes for a moment. Then she took a deep breath and said, "The essence of the Dharma is the same as Truth."

Asanga reflected on her words. He was accustomed to this style of informal philosophical debate, so he came up with a suitable rejoinder.

"That is what Truth has become. It is not Truth because it is true, but because it captures the essence of the Dharma we believe to be true."

"That is what Maitreya has done!"

"But who is Maitreya?" Asanga said insistently

Buddhi turned away, refusing to answer.

They sat in silence for several minutes, not looking at each other. Asanga felt satisfied that he got as much information as he could from this initial meeting, but not nearly as much as he needed. He got up from the log and stood in front of her.

"I will visit you again soon."

"If you must," she said while getting up slowly from the ground.

Looking him in the eye, she added, "Truth does not live in the biographical, but in what is true regardless of who professes it."

VII

Asanga stayed at the hermitage on the hill, keeping to his tiny room throughout the rest of the day and night. He sat in meditation for several hours, changing his posture every thirty minutes or so. His thoughts first circled around what it meant if the true identity of the author of Maitreya's verses was a woman. He worried about that becoming known. If that were to happen, it could discredit Maitreya's teachings and bring shame upon him.

Asanga could see no diplomatic way to retract these teachings if it became known that a woman had created them. He decided he must stand behind Maitreya's teachings no matter what. But that stance made him more like a Mara and less like a bodhisattva. Then, his mind plunged into a state of anguish like he had never known before, and out of that despair he succumbed to the belief that he had lived for the counterfeit Dharma and not the true Dharma.

It was at this very low point of feeling that Asanga recalled the story of the Buddha's prophecy. The Buddha's personal attendant and chronicler, Ananda, had pleaded with the Buddha to allow women into the Sangha. Ananda persisted despite the Buddha's opposition. When the Buddha finally acquiesced, he predicted that the Dharma would last only five hundred years, whereas before it would have lasted for a thousand. All because women were permitted to shave their heads, wear the robes of a bhikshu, and take on additional rules.

Asanga contemplated the story of the Buddha's prophecy throughout the night. He reasoned that if it was a prediction about his present situation, then he should be able to understand it in a way no one has before. As he turned the story around in his mind, lining it up with the events in his life, a realization arose, giving birth to a new interpretation of the Buddha's prophecy.

Women were permitted to enter the Sangha. The Dharma went through several transformations for five hundred years until the true meaning of the Buddha's words were lost, though the words remained, which ended the allotted period for someone to attain nirvana within Gautama Buddha's Dharma dispensation. Counterfeit teachings were then propagated for a few hundred years, creating confusion in the minds of many as to what the Buddha originally meant. Then, because Ananda persuaded the Buddha to allow women into the Sangha, a bhikshuni was born who became the carrier of the teachings of the next Buddha, Maitreya. It made perfect sense to Asanga that a woman would do this, for why else would the prophecy be intrinsically connected with the formation of the Bhikshuni Sangha?

Asanga was certain that what he understood was the real story. He no longer saw himself as a Mara, but once again as a bodhisattva who was destined to spread the teaching of the next Buddha, Maitreya. Asanga felt compelled to learn more about Buddhi. He had to figure out why she was the one to bring Maitreya's teachings to him. There must be something special about her.

On alms round, Asanga decided to eat his food sitting on the log in front of Buddhi's hut. As he was finishing his meal, Buddhi and her companion bhikshuni returned from their alms round. They appeared embarrassed by the sight of a bhikshu waiting for them, and so hurriedly went into the hut and shut the door. Asanga was not dismayed by this response. He went back to the village to clean his alms bowl and wash up at a nearby well. When that was done, he sat down at the foot of a banyan tree and meditated for an hour. Then he went back to the log in front of Buddhi's hut and waited patiently for her to come out.

She finally emerged, ignoring Asanga as she walked down to the stream not far from her hut. Asanga watched her as she walked back to the hut and beckoned her to sit on the ground a few feet from him.

"You have returned as promised," Buddhi said.

"There are things I need to know."

She did not say a word, but looked in his eyes, curiously.

"Tell me about your life," Asanga said.

She cringed at his request. She did not want to comply, but Asanga pleaded with her, saying that the future of Maitreya's teachings depends on him knowing the full story about their origin. Only then will he be able to trust his intuition that it is the true Dharma prophesied by the Buddha.

Buddhi relented and said, "It is as I said before. But let me say it again differently because you have failed to understand. If a teaching captures the essence of the Buddha's teaching, then it can be said to be the Dharma. Who taught it is irrelevant!"

"You sound like my brother, Vasubandhu," he said. And I happen to agree with his assessment, except I would not have gone so far as to say that a person's history is irrelevant, for it can provide insights into the mind of the person claiming to speak the true teaching, and thus assist in detecting the flaws inherent in that teaching.

Asanga then said, "I can never know with absolute conviction who created these new teachings. I will always have to take it on faith that it was Maitreya. But I believe I can understand the events that have unfolded around these teachings better if I could know something about the person who recited them."

"I see," she said. "Your brother, Vasubandhu, is that famous bhikshu, the victor in all debates. He gives credence to the notion that Container Consciousness is both individual and universal, which lends support to the idea you use to persuade me to speak of my life. But, I am not so easily convinced."

"Then let me give you an example," Asanga said. "A revered teacher of unparalleled wisdom teaches thousands of students the doctrine of momentariness. He lays bare the whole edifice of the Abhidharma, giving his students a deep and penetrating analysis of the human mind. Then, one day, he decides to prove his theories by observing his mind in meditation and discovers that what he has been teaching is inaccurate and flawed. Thus, it is through awareness of our subjective reality that concepts about ultimate reality come into question.

"Now, as I understand Maitreya's view, ultimate reality is based on the innermost subjectivity, Consciousness-Only. So, a person's story is intrinsically connected with that person's truth, and her truth is dependent on her mind, which, in turn, perceives and thinks in accordance with the seeds of karma."

"You will not hear my life story! Not from me!"

Buddhi then jumped up from the ground and ran inside the hut, shutting the door behind her.

Asanga despaired that he would never hear her story. He regretted not bringing me along. But how could he know before-hand what he was going find on this seemingly innocent journey? He briefly considered returning home and asking me to join him, but dropped that notion after giving it some thought. He did not want anyone to know this side of Maitreya's story, not even his trustworthy brother.

While he was lost in thought, the door to the hut opened and the other bhikshuni appeared. She walked over to Asanga, bowed once, and then sat on the ground in front of him.

She said, "Buddhi told me why you are here and what you want from her. She asked me to relate her life story. She cannot go through the anguish of telling it again. It is her former life of torment, ridicule, and oppression that reminds her that liberation for herself alone is not true liberation at all."

VIII

The conversation that followed between Asanga and the other bhikshuni lasted until sunset. I need not repeat everything Asanga recounted to me several years after the fact. A condensed version will suffice.

Buddhi was the only daughter of a brahmin priest. She had three brothers, two older and one younger. Her father was a strict observer of the laws of *Manu*. He attempted to teach her eldest brother the *Vedas* and *Puranas* when he was a young boy in anticipation of him becoming a master of sacrifices, hymns, and ceremonies when he was of age. The eldest son, Arjuna, began his education at the age of five, just after Buddhi was born. He was a rambunctious boy who loved to play in the woods. Their father forced him to sit much of the day, teaching him verses to memorize. He envied his younger brother, Kavi, who played games and ran through the fields with the other boys in the village.

As Arjuna neared the age of ten, he was taught how to read and write. By that time, Buddhi was five and the youngest son was two. Buddhi liked to sit in on her brother's lessons. Within a year, she was able to read Sanskrit and write down verses she heard her father recite. She had learned without difficulty the lessons her eldest brother was supposed to have mastered. Their father basically ignored her achievements, while at the same time pressuring Arjuna to study harder. Instead of becoming a better student, Arjuna became resentful, turning his rage in the direction of his precocious sister, calling her names and hitting her when no adults were around.

Buddhi's father eventually forbade her from studying. She was restricted to helping her mother with the cleaning and cooking. But she could overhear her father reciting the Vedas and was able to dedicate them to memory within a year while doing her other chores. She had to keep her learning a secret, especially from her father and brothers, so she would volunteer to lead the family cow to graze in the morning, where she would sit under a tree and recite sacred verses. Other cowherds, mostly young boys, began to tease her. The rest joined in and she was mocked by all the boys in the village, who knew her brothers, and soon her secret was out.

Her father strictly forbade her from learning. Under no condition was she to recite the Vedas or any other scripture. It was not for girls. Meanwhile, Arjuna, nearing thirteen, had enough of this brahmanical education and rebelled against their father, striking him down in a fight, and then fleeing the village, never to return. He was forever cursed by their father, who now put all his faith in the youngest son.

This choice proved more troublesome than the first, for the youngest, named Rama, who was not even seven years of age, was not very bright. He was an even slower learner than Arjuna. Their father lost his temper often, yelling at the poor boy. Buddhi cowered in fear at her father and tried not to aggravate him.

By her tenth year, her father had arranged a marriage for her to a respectable brahmin youth in a neighboring village. She had heard rumors that this boy, who was fifteen, Arjuna's age, was arrogant and cruel. He loved to perform bloody sacrifices to the gods and was proud of his skill with the blade. Buddhi loved animals and tended them when sick or injured.

Then one day, a few weeks after the marriage contract was agreed upon, though before the first installment of her dowry was sent to the groom's family, Buddhi was outside milking the family cow when a female mendicant appeared, silently begging for alms. It was the first time Buddhi had seen a woman shrouded in white and wearing a cloth rag over her mouth.

Buddhi asked her so many questions, that the woman, who was a Jain nun of the *svetambara* sect, invited Buddhi to come with her to a Jain temple, where all her questions would be answered by those wiser than herself. Buddhi stopped milking the cow and walked away with the female mendicant, never telling her parents.

I found this part of the story hard to believe. Surely a young girl would tell her parents before walking away with a stranger. But I gathered that this story covered up a more painful reality, one which Buddhi had probably never revealed to anyone.

Buddhi quickly mastered the essentials of the Jain doctrine. She wanted to be ordained as a Jain nun, but was forced to wait, since she was needed as a temple helper. The work around the temple required excessive physical labor, and she soon found herself too exhausted at the end of the day to do much memorizing. This went on for a couple of years and she pleaded daily with the *nirgranthas* to ordain her as one of their own, so that she could immerse herself in the study of their doctrine.

In response to her pleas, at the age of twelve, she was given the opportunity to travel with a small group of Jain nuns to Pataliputra, where a larger Jain community might be able to take her in and ordain her. On the second night of their journey, the Jain nuns set up camp not far from a group of five bhikshus. Buddhi had never seen bhikshus before, which surprised the nirgranthas, for they contemptuously saw bhikshus and bhikshunis everywhere. Before dawn, Buddhi was awakened by the bhikshus preparing to leave. Being curious, she asked one of the bhikshus to tell her about the Buddha's teaching. From just hearing a few words, she was convinced that the Dharma was the Truth. She decided to quit the Jains and accompany the five bhikshus to a monastery that had a separate building for bhikshunis. She lived there as an *anagarika* (homeless ten-precept holder) and studied tirelessly until she reached the age of ordination. During the time period before becoming a fully ordained bhikshuni, Buddhi had supposedly mastered the Tripitaka and several Mahayana Sutras. That is an amazing feat for any man. She also trained her mind in logic and meditated for several hours a day.

Even after hearing this story, Asanga still believed that Buddhi was just a human vehicle used to carry the teachings of Maitreya and was not their author.

As I write these last words in my commentary on the life of Maitreya, there is no way to ascertain who composed these teachings. Or is there?

For the first time since I heard this story, I wonder if Buddhi is still alive. Asanga only said that Maitreya can no longer be found in any realm of existence. Asanga never said the same of the woman who gave voice to Maitreya's teachings and who may even be their creator.

Vasubandhu's Search for Maitreya

IX

Vasubandhu walks with accelerated purpose on his way to the royal palace. The king must grant him leave. The fate of the Buddha's teaching now rests on Vasubandhu's shoulders. But he knows he must act fast. He quickens his pace, and were he not a bhikshu, he would most certainly be running.

While Vasubandhu's physical form is statuesque, his brow is lined and furrowed by over seventy years of the most arduous types of thinking. He perceives his mind moving sixteen times faster than his body, for he believes that is a universal law, laid down in the Abhidharma. A physical moment might typically reveal these sixteen thoughts:

Buddhi is Maitreya.
Buddhi may still be alive.
Only Buddhi can clarify,
Teach,
Expound,
Dispense,
Exemplify that teaching.

Buddhi may be a fraud,
A mere scholar,
A Mara.
Only Vasubandhu, the Great Scholar, can determine which.
The future of the Dharma depends on him.
The Dharma is true regardless of all of this.
He must separate the true from the counterfeit.
Only by meeting Buddhi will this happen.
How can any of this be proved?

The last thought is then grasped with a tight grip. This is natural for his mind, which, as an organ of conceptualization, keeps moving in and out of flux, gripping and then releasing one prominent thought after another. In this way, he ingests each of these thoughts, and is then able to store them within his vast consciousness as seeds for future karma. This is how he fashions the world according to his thoughts. But Vasubandhu does not make the mistake of identifying with his thoughts, for he is the void where thought cannot enter. That is what he believes. Though, when asked, he tends to take this conceptualization a step further: *Everything is of the void and yet the void itself is empty of everything.*

But he does not speak this way to the unenlightened. He lets them know that he is a bhikshu dedicated to serving the poor and infirm, who humbly requires gifts to establish hospitals, orphanages, schools, and monasteries.

King Vikramaditya employs Vasubandhu as the crown prince's personal teacher. It is in this capacity that he addresses the palace guards, who allow to him pass through the gate.

It is unusual for Vasubandhu to visit the king before the morning meal, which is when King Vikramaditya is usually in the assembly hall granting audiences, dispensing verdicts, or conferring with his generals. Because of the king's morning meetings, the soldiers guarding the doors to the assembly hall refuse to let Vasubandhu enter. So, he paces back and forth in the hallway for eight cycles, and then asks the guards to let him in.

The chief officer of the palace guards tells Vasubandhu to wait in the garden until King Vikramaditya summons him. While he walks about the garden, Vasubandhu considers his current state of urgency. Time is not entirely real. There is only the present moment. The past no longer exists and the future has yet to exist. Only in a conventional sense can time be said to be real, especially when applied to old age and death. And it is the reality of old age and death that makes what he intends to do of the utmost urgency.

Because of that last thought, he goes back to the assembly hall and demands to be let in. The guards ignore him. Fortunately, only a few moments pass before the doors open to the assembly hall and out walk the king's generals, who move aside as Vasubandhu dashes into the hall. The crown prince is standing by his father's side and is the first to notice Vasubandhu's surprise entrance. To cover for his teacher's breach of protocol, the prince whispers in his father's ear as a way of announcing Vasubandhu's unexpected presence. King Vikramaditya rises from his throne and walks over to Vasubandhu, who now stands in the center of the hall with guards and onlookers on the periphery.

King Vikramaditya is a muscular man who wears a kindly expression on what is otherwise an ugly face. It has always struck Vasubandhu as incongruous that such a hideous looking king would love philosophy and choose to be a patron of the needy, the homeless, and the infirm. Besides the king's compassion for his subjects, he possesses a ready mind, and has always crowned Vasubandhu the victor in debates.

King Vikramaditya says, "What brings you here so early in the day? Is it something to do with the prince's education?"

Vasubandhu says, "I must beg you to grant me leave to travel to the northern-most reaches of the kingdom."

"What will then become of my son's instruction?" King Vikramaditya says. "May he join you on this journey?"

Vasubandhu is puzzled by the king's request.

"It may not be the kind of journey suited to the prince's current studies."

"Let me decide that!" King Vikramaditya says, his temper showing. "Tell me, Vasubandhu, what is the purpose of your journey?"

Vasubandhu cannot lie and yet he cannot bring himself to reveal the whole story. For a moment, he regrets coming to the king in the first place and wishes he would have just left on his own without telling anyone. But he cannot make such a journey without King Vikramaditya's blessing. If Vasubandhu just disappeared one day, the king would send soldiers to look for him and bring him back. He is more than just an ordinary subject. Vasubandhu, the undefeatable debater, is a prized possession.

Vasubandhu says, "Today I finished writing my commentary on the life of Maitreya as told to me by my late brother, Asanga."

"That must be a fascinating story!" King Vikramaditya says, his mood shifting to something more pleasant. "But what does your journey have to do with Asanga and Maitreya?"

"As I was writing the last words to my commentary, I realized that the person who may have authored Maitreya's teachings could still be alive. And, this person would be very advanced in years. That is why I must leave immediately."

"That is most intriguing!"

King Vikramaditya glances at his son to share his curiosity at this revelation.

The prince says, "I am curious. Who is the real Maitreya?"

Vasubandhu wishes he did not have to answer the prince's question, but he must.

"I cannot say for certain. That is why I must find this person. Only then can I determine the true authorship of Maitreya's teachings."

King Vikramaditya says, "How will you be able to determine that?"

"Through debate, of course."

"But surely it will take much more than an exchange of ideas to determine if this person is indeed Maitreya. I have an idea. Why not take a group of men capable of judging the authenticity of this individual?"

The prince says, "That is an excellent idea! I would like to be one of them."

"I would like to go also," the king says, "but I am afraid I cannot travel at this time. Our western borders are threatened. Vasubandhu, I will give you the charge of my son and will appoint horses and men to accompany you. I will choose the two other judges."

"Thank you. That is most generous. But, may I differ on one point?" Vasubandhu says, careful to be respectful. "I am the only person truly capable of determining the legitimacy of the author of Maitreya's works and need no help in that regard."

King Vikramaditya adopts a stern, worldly wise tone with Vasubandhu. "You are certainly a capable man when it comes to debating, Vasubandhu. But I am afraid your psychic powers are limited. I will arrange for a sadhu who possesses the ability to know the thoughts of other beings. I will also have one of my trusted ministers accompany you. He is a man skilled in uncovering the deceits and craftiness of others. If all of you agree that this person is indeed Maitreya, then there can be no room for doubt."

X

Two full days pass before Vasubandhu's three companions are ready to depart in search of Buddhi. Vasubandhu finds this delay to be particularly aggravating. He cannot sleep at night, mulling over in his mind why he has been blind to Buddhi's existence for all these years.

The sadhu and the minister are the ones responsible for the delay. The sadhu, who is the head of the Samkhya sect, must perform a series of rituals before setting off. He fasts and bathes, makes sacrifices and offerings, chants and meditates until he knows he is prepared to embark on this sacred mission. King Vikramaditya's generous donation for his services motivates him as well.

The minister needs additional time to brief his subordinates on their responsibilities while he is away. Even when the four men meet outside the palace gates with their retinue, the minister requests more time to attend to details left unfinished. Vasubandhu, the avowed leader of the group, denies the minister's request. The minister is not accustomed to being treated disrespectfully by a bhikshu, and so demands that Vasubandhu allow him to speak to his replacement one last time. Vasubandhu orders all of them to mount their horses.

They look like a group of misfits as they ride through the countryside. The sadhu is a slim man, middle-aged, with long wavy gray hair. It is his first time riding a horse. He wears only a white *lungi* that strangles his groin as he rides bareback.

The minister is an elder statesman, of the warrior caste, who was a captain in the army as a young man and an ambassador in his middle years. Though his hair is white and his face full of wrinkles, he rides his horse with the strength of a much younger man. He occasionally brings his horse even with Vasubandhu, who rides in the lead, but then pulls back, remembering how the bhikshu rebuffed him earlier.

The prince hangs back, taking in the scenery. He has a young page riding near him, and they often remark on the trees, the birds, and the occasional wild animal. At one point his young servant believes he sees a lion, but that is quickly dismissed upon taking a prolonged look at the creature in the distance, which turns out to be a jackal.

Vasubandhu rides in front, his back straight and his eyes focused on the narrow horse path in front of him. He knows this path better than anyone else, having traveled it often. There is a shortcut through the jungle several miles to the north, but he does not mention it, since it is only traversable on foot.

That evening, after they have arrived at the house of a village chieftain, the four of them have their first formal meeting.

The minister speaks first, presenting his plan for tracking down Buddhi and bringing her in for questioning. He suggests sending out a spy to watch her movements, so that they can determine the right time and place to kidnap her. Once they have captured her, they then bring her to a house and lock her in a room. First they starve her, and then they interrogate her. That is the only way the minister can trust what she says.

The sadhu finds the minister's plan appalling. He proposes that one of them goes up to her disguised as a beggar, or, better yet, a cripple, so as to gain her sympathy. Once inside her hut and under her care, he can then use his psychic powers to determine her authenticity.

Vasubandhu says, "I have another plan. I suggest all four of us look for her. When we find out where she is staying, I invite her to a public feast. At this gathering, we ask her questions in public. That is sure to bring truthful answers. No bhikshuni would ever deceive others in public."

The minister says, "Why would she not lie to us?"

"It would be a grave offense, one that she would have to confess. Since she does not know what my brother Asanga has told me, she will have to tell me the truth. If she deviates from what I know from my brother to be true, I will have caught her in a lie."

The sadhu says, "But would she not feel attacked by us?"

"I assure you," Vasubandhu says, "that if she is indeed Maitreya, she will be calm and composed, and will answer all of our questions honestly. If she is not Maitreya, we can anticipate less friendly behavior."

The prince says, "If she is indeed Maitreya, then this strategy may not be necessary. Why not ask her, when we find her, if she is Maitreya?"

"Because," Vasubandhu says, with irritation, "it is not up to her to make that claim."

"I agree," the minister says.

"So, are we agreed on our plan?" Vasubandhu says.

They all assent. The minister and the sadhu go to their rooms for the night.

Vasubandhu asks the prince to stay a moment longer.

"I have a task for you," he says.

"What may that be?"

"I need you to watch our two companions very closely. Tell to me what they say. Observe how they act."

"Why is that?"

"If I am to consider their opinions in this matter, I need to know more about them than they are willing to tell me. It must be understood that you will never reveal what I have asked of you."

The prince says, "I will be so natural and subtle that they will never suspect I am observing them."

XI

During the next three days of their journey, the prince engages both the sadhu and the minister in a series of conversations. The prince discovers much that he deems useful. For instance, the minister gets quite animated when talking about the battles he led as a young captain for the prince's grandfather. It was not the close combat that the minister fondly recollects, for he had no real taste for shedding blood, but the strategic deployment of soldiers under his command. Not one battle was lost, and the kingdom expanded, becoming in his estimation, even larger than it was in Emperor Ashoka's day. Strategizing is the minister's special skill.

The sadhu mostly speaks of his life in terms of fasts and holy pilgrimages. He once fasted for four weeks. Lord Krishna first appeared to him in the guise of a young cowherd and offered to teach him the law of Maya, but the sadhu was holding out for something more practical. Two days later, Lord Shiva appeared to him as a beggar, offering him the power to know the minds of others and see their destinations beyond this life. That would be of more use to him, so he took it.

When the prince, deciding to the test the sadhu's psychic powers, asks the sadhu to tell him what he is thinking, the sadhu smiles and says, "It does not work like that."

The conversations are not merely one-sided, as the prince is a conduit of information regarding Maitreya's teaching. When the sadhu asks the prince to tell him the specifics of Maitreya's teaching, he interrupts the prince, going off on a rant about the tendency of Buddhist philosophers to indulge in needless complexity, when all they need to realize is that the One is the cause of everything, sustains all the worlds, and destroys it all in the end. The minister, upon only hearing the rudiments of Maitreya's teaching, unequivocally states that it is the most preposterous philosophy he has ever heard.

Vasubandhu enjoys relative isolation for those three days, riding alone in front, sleeping in his own separate room when they stop for the night. He contemplates various assertions found in Maitreya's teaching and is determined not to let the outcome of this journey persuade him to doubt their validity, for he has verified them several times over. When he fantasizes about debating Buddhi, he pictures her as a healthy, attractive woman in her seventies, with a sharp intellect and impeccable memory, essentially a female version of himself.

On the fifth day of their journey, they arrive at the palace of the vassal king of this region. They enter the palace courtyard as the morning meal is being served. They dismount and join the gathered guests.

Vasubandhu sits on a long bench with thirty other bhikshus; the prince sits on a cushioned chair at a table with the king and other noblemen; the sadhu sits on the ground with other half-naked ascetics; and the minister joins his counterpart at the far end of the king's table. Each of them feels at home in the company of their peers.

Vasubandhu gets to work gathering useful information. He finds out that a bhikshuni resembling Buddhi lives in a village to the north. A young bhikshu volunteers to lead Vasubandhu there. They must wait till morning however, as the journey is too long to be accomplished in a single afternoon, even though Vasubandhu wants to leave right away.

After a couple of hours spent conversing with their peers, Vasubandhu, the prince, the minister, and the sadhu meet to go over their plan for tomorrow. They all agree that once they arrive in Buddhi's village, they will split up. The sadhu will seek out other sadhus and ask them what they know about Buddhi. The minister will consult the village chieftain regarding Buddhi, as well as arrange a feast in honor of Vasubandhu's visit. The prince will be disguised as a beggar and mingle with the people in town, finding out all he can. While Vasubandhu will visit the hermitage outside the village and ask the bhikshus questions about her.

The only person concerned about his role is the prince.

"How can being a beggar make the villagers talk to me? I thought the common folk despise beggars."

Vasubandhu says, "A beggar is the perfect disguise. I have used it many times with superb results. No one suspects a person in rags to have any standing in society. If he belonged to one of the higher castes, he would be well-groomed and properly dressed."

"So," the prince says, "they will say anything to a beggar, thinking that he is not a person. Should I act as if I am mad?"

"That has additional advantages, if you can pull it off. But, in this scenario, it might make people less willing to talk to you."

The prince says, "I see Vasubandhu's plan most clearly now. Listen to me for a moment."

"Yes, your majesty," the minister says.

"Chieftains, sadhus, bhikshus, and the common folk do not speak honestly outside of their groups. A nobleman will not speak openly to a commoner, a bhikshu will not reveal privileged information except to another bhikshu, a sadhu treats a devotee differently than another sadhu, and the submissive villagers will only speak freely when there is no authority present. That is the beauty of Vasubandhu's plan to gather intelligence." Then turning to the minister, the prince adds, "I am surprised that you have not used such tactics."

The minister says, "I have used spies, but not in this way. I see your point, young prince, and consider this to be a sound plan."

"Then we are agreed," Vasubandhu says. "We shall soon know if Buddhi is indeed Maitreya."

XII

The four of them set out at dawn, with the young bhikshu as their guide, arriving in the afternoon.

They enter the village individually, except for Vasubandhu and the young bhikshu, who walk through the village to a hermitage situated on a small hill. There they find five bhikshus who seem to observing a vow of silence as none of them will answer Vasubandhu's questions. Then Vasubandhu realizes that this the same hermitage Asanga told him about. So Buddhi's hut must be just off the path they just took to get there. He must have passed it. Vasubandhu retraces his steps back to town and finds the tiny hut with a large log in front of it. Vasubandhu sits down on the log and considers his next move.

He hears some men approaching, shouting at the top of their lungs. They are chasing after someone. It is the prince disguised as a beggar. Vasubandhu thought he had made it perfectly clear that the prince was not to steal anything. The prince runs past Vasubandhu and winks at him. At that moment, Vasubandhu hears a woman's voice speak to him from the hut.

Vasubandhu turns around and sees a bent-over bhikshuni standing outside the hut. He gets up and walks over to her. She bows before him as he remains standing. When she rises, she asks, "Why are you here?"

He says, "To meet all those who profess the teachings of Maitreya. Are you not one who proclaims those teachings?"

"I do not proclaim the teachings of Maitreya. You must have me mixed up with another bhikshuni."

Vasubandhu senses her reticence and knows he must push past it if he is to get anywhere.

"Come join me for a Dharma conversation. Here on this log."

Vasubandhu walks over to the log and sits down on it.

She remains standing.

"I do not engage in frivolous talk," she says. "Who are you?"

"Come join me and I will tell you what you need to know."

"I am old, but I can hear well enough from here. I ask you again. Who are you?"

Vasubandhu pauses a moment to consider whether to come up with a false name or tell the truth. Now, if he can only say his name and nothing more.

"My name is Vasubandhu."

"That is all I need to know," she says.

Buddhi hobbles over to the log. Instead of sitting on the ground, she sits down on the opposite end of the log.

"I have difficulty standing up when sitting on the ground. Please do not take this as disrespect."

"I am still seated a finger-width higher," Vasubandhu says, smiling at her.

"You said you wanted to discuss the Dharma. What have you to say?"

"It is not what I have to say that has brought me here," says Vasubandhu, "but what I wish to ask."

The bhikshuni closes her eyes and seems to fall asleep. He briefly considers waking her, but then decides it is better to let her sleep.

As they sit there on the log, the sadhu walks up the road and stops opposite them. He stands and stares at Buddhi as she sleeps. Vasubandhu gets up and walks over to the him.

"What have you found out?"

The sadhu says, "She is known as a recluse of little wants, no friends. She possesses magical powers. And I sense that she is now in a deep samadhi. I believe she has everything one would expect to find in a truly liberated sage."

Vasubandhu glances over at her and then at the sadhu.

"I am quite sure she is asleep. Is that what you Hindus call samadhi?"

The sadhu says, "You are obviously not an adept. For, if you were, you would know that samadhi and sleep are two sides of the same coin."

The last thing Vasubandhu wants to do is get into a debate with the sadhu. So, he yields this point to the sadhu, much to the yogi's satisfaction. The sadhu walks away smiling, while Vasubandhu silently returns to the log, sitting down where he was before.

Vasubandhu now focuses his attention on the bhikshuni's outward appearance. She seems much older than he imagined, more like a hundred years old. Her skin is dry and wrinkled, having conquered her facial features completely, making her look nothing like Asanga's description.

He then hears her gasp for air, as if she had been holding her breath underwater. This alarms him, but he does nothing except stare at her, waiting for some sign that she is still alive. Then he notices a radiance in her eyes and a glow about her skin. In the instantaneous span of sixteen mind moments, Vasubandhu's consciousness registers the face Asanga saw.

Returning to her hundred-year-old form, she says, "You are Asanga's brother."

"How do you know am I not another Vasubandhu?"

"Who else would travel such a long distance to ask me about the teachings of Maitreya?"

"So you know why I am here?"

"Karma," she says, with a chuckle.

Vasubandhu chuckles at her attempt at Buddhist humor.

"Your karma or my karma?"

"It is all the same," she says.

"We are all interconnected."

"No," she says, "that is not it."

"Then what is it?"

"What you have done and what I have done have led us to this moment."

Vasubandhu says, "You must come to a feast held in my honor tomorrow. If what we have done has led to this moment, then what we do in this moment will lead to what we do in future moments."

Buddhi gets up from the log, gradually straightening her back as she stands, even though she ends up severely hunched over. She shuffles to face him.

"Have your beggar friend come get me when it is time."

XIII

Vasubandhu sits at the head of a row of about ten bhikshus. Buddhi is seated at the other end of the row. The laypeople are seated in rows facing the bhikshus and the lone bhikshuni. In the front row are the prince, the sadhu, and the minister.

Behind them sits the chieftain, his family, and other villagers of high birth. In the outer row are merchants and laborers.

All the bhikshus, including Buddhi, are served first, and only then is everyone else allowed to partake. After everyone has eaten, Vasubandhu speaks to the whole assembly.

"Today, we have gathered for the purpose of learning the truth about Maitreya's teachings. I will be asking questions of the bhikshuni, Buddhi."

The minister rises from his seat to request that Vasubandhu and Buddhi sit in the center of the hall. The bhikshus move back to make space for Vasubandhu to sit facing Buddhi. Once everyone is settled, Vasubandhu addresses Buddhi directly.

"What are the core teachings of Maitreya?"

Buddhi says, "I am not accustomed to speaking to such assemblies, so please forgive an old woman her shaky voice. I do not know why I should be the one to answer these questions, since our esteemed guest, Venerable Vasubandhu, has written many commentaries on the teachings of Maitreya."

She coughs twice and then it seems as though an invisible being has taken over her body.

She says, "Whatever you believe to be true is a belief that can be looked at from a variety of angles. And, if it is true from every angle, then it is no longer a belief in what is true but is what is true. The Dharma is known in all ways, and in all worlds, as the true teaching of liberation for all beings."

Vasubandhu is intrigued by this conceptualization, but he does not have time to examine it closely. Instead, he asks, "Where is this teaching found in Maitreya's verses?"

Buddhi apparently enters a mild trance and then speaks in a monotone.

"Basic reality, characteristic reality, the reality that is non-reversal, the reality which consists of fruition and its cause, more subtle and gross realities, the examined and accepted, the characteristic of differentiation, the ten-fold reality of skillful means, and the antidotes to the view of self."

Vasubandhu is stunned to hear this list of realities found in Maitreya's verses on distinguishing the middle from the extremes.

Now his mind can comprehend the deeper truth found in her previous answer. These are the realities that both define the Dharma and are true at the same time.

Vasubandhu relishes this realization for less time than he would like. Instead, he acts on the pressure he feels to keep the interrogation going forward.

"What is liberation?"

Buddhi's face now appears as if she has been transported back in time half a century.

She says, "By liberation, do you mean emptiness? Or do you mean nothing more to be done?"

"Are they not the same?" Vasubandhu says.

"Emptiness is not the end of suffering when there is still something to be done. When there is nothing to be done, that is liberation. The liberated consciousness may enter into emptiness, but it is not defined by it."

"Then," Vasubandhu says, "which vehicle are you referring to, the Mahayana or the Hinayana?"

"Both!" Buddhi says. "But with one distinction. Liberation in the Mahayana is doing that which will someday lead to nothing more to be done, while for arhats, liberation is the end of doing."

Vasubandhu pauses a moment to assess how this is going. He honestly feels no closer to determining if Buddhi is Maitreya than he was before meeting her. He acknowledges that she is giving him some highly provocative ideas, which he would like to memorize for future commentaries, but that is not his mission here. He concludes that he cannot confirm that Buddhi is Maitreya from this line of questioning. He must be more direct.

Vasubandhu says, "Tell me, where does Maitreya's teaching come from? Who created It?"

Buddhi seems perplexed by these two questions.

While she sits silently, Vasubandhu speaks to the whole assembly.

"As a bhikshuni bound by the vow to always tell the truth, tell us, who is the author of Maitreya's verses?"

When her voice returns, it sounds to Vasubandhu as though Asanga is speaking through her.

"Maitreya's teaching comes from Venerable Asanga meeting the bodhisattva in his twelve years in the forest."

"Who did Asanga get Maitreya's verses from?" Vasubandhu says, pressing her to reveal more.

"From Maitreya!"

"But who is Maitreya?"

She raises her eyes to meet Vasubandhu's gaze squarely.

"I am Maitreya! Asanga is Maitreya! Dhira, our teacher, is Maitreya!"

"How can the three of you be Maitreya?"

A commotion ensues, with everyone talking at once.

Buddhi leans forward and whispers something that only Vasubandhu can hear. Then she gets up and walks out, leaving Vasubandhu sitting alone in the center of the room.

The prince jumps up from his seat and orders everyone to be quiet.

He says, "Tell us the truth, Vasubandhu. Is she Maitreya?"

Vasubandhu replies, "That is not for me alone to decide. Let the four of us confer in private."

XIV

Vasubandhu, The prince, the sadhu, and the minister go to an empty room in the large house. They sit at four points on a diamond, with the prince facing Vasubandhu and the sadhu and minister opposite each other.

The minister says, "I have made up my mind. I cannot say that she is Maitreya."

The sadhu says, "I share the minister's conclusion."

The crown prince says, "I say she is Maitreya!"

Vasubandhu looks at the prince and wonders how the young man could reach such a conclusion. Has Vasubandhu not taught him to be more discerning?

"It is your enthusiasm, young prince, that leads you to this conclusion. Not reason, not facts."

The prince says, "Then, what are the facts? What does reason tell you?"

Vasubandhu says, "You heard what Buddhi said. Asanga, Dhira, and Buddhi are the authors of Maitreya's verses. But, how did they compose them? It was not by ordinary means. That is what she told me."

The minister says, "Tell us what she said."

Vasubandhu tries to speak, but keeps stopping himself as if what he is about to say will lose him the debate.

Finally, Vasubandhu comes out with it.

"The three of them channeled Maitreya."

"Is that possible? Are you certain? Are you crazy?" They say all at once, starting with the prince and ending with the minister.

"No!" Vasubandhu says. "But we must leave it at that. Buddhi can, at best, be one of the three authors of Maitreya's teachings. There is no evidence to conclude that she is Maitreya."

"Agreed!"

XV

Vasubandhu decides to leave early in the morning before the others are awake. This is a journey he must embark on alone. He carries his few belongings wrapped in a cloth that is tied to a long staff balanced on his right shoulder.

Once he leaves the foothills, the land is flat with expanses of cultivated fields and wild marshes obscured by the mid-morning fog. As his eyes try to see through the fog around him, his inward vision sees his mind as shifting vapor dependent on, yet distinct from, his body. He stands still and thinks to himself.

Dependent on earth, moisture, temperature, and sunlight, mist arises. Upon mist being so, obscuration comes to be. With obscuration present, there is no seeing clearly. When there is no seeing clearly, one can easily lose one's way and fall victim to misfortune.

Then Vasubandhu takes a few cautious steps forward. He hopes he will not stumble and hurt himself. He suddenly becomes acutely aware of his advanced years, his failing abilities, his uncertainty about the rest of his life and what lies in wait for him when this life ends.

When the sun heats the moist land, the mist grows stronger before evaporating completely. Only upon evaporation, does seeing clearly become possible.

A crow caws from a nearby tree and Vasubandhu turns his head in that direction. He cannot see the crow sitting on the mist-shrouded branch, but he is certain that even though he does not see it, it is there. He squints and tries to see through the fog to find the crow in the tree, but all he sees is an impenetrable wall of gray.

To believe in what one imagines to be real is not real knowledge. Yet there is always something real in the imagined, since what is real is not entirely distinct from the imagined.

There first must be haze for there to be clarity.
Without one, how could the other come to be?

Maitreya

XVI

"L et us not give It a name," Buddhi says in response to an attempt by Asanga to speak in a defining manner.

"Then how is It to be communicated?" Asanga asks.

"Why must we communicate It?" Buddhi says.

"So that others may benefit."

"Is that what we are talking about? Spreading the Dharma?"

"Always."

"Then," she says, "let us definitely not give It a name!"

At the time this conversation takes place, Asanga is in his twelfth and last year alone in the forest. As you can see, he is far from alone. A year earlier, he was introduced to Buddhi at a festival held in honor of the Buddha's parinirvana. The bhikshu who introduced them was no other than the old toothless bhikshu, known as Dhira, "The Wise One."

Dhira met Asanga on alms round a year prior to this conversation, the last of many that will occur between Asanga and Buddhi. Buddhi was Dhira's most advanced student, and he was eager to introduce her to Asanga. After spending only a few minutes with Asanga, he sensed that Buddhi and Asanga were much on the same path, which Dhira paradoxically calls, "The

Path of Confusion." He would often remind them both that only through the confusing nature of mind is self abandoned; and, when there is no self, confusion vanishes like a flame snuffed out.

A year ago, when the three of them first met, they had this conversation.

"What is left when the self is abandoned?" Asanga asked.

"That which is not held onto," Dhira replied.

"Then it is the extinguishing of the Grasper and the Grasped. A nondual emptiness. Am I right?"

"Note what he does," Buddhi said to Dhira. "He puts into words what cannot fit into words."

"Or perhaps," Dhira said to her, "he has truly understood."

Dhira often feels waves of joy at the discussions between Asanga and Buddhi. They prompt him to consider how he would talk about the meditative states he has experienced. Surely, Buddhi and Asanga would understand him if he is able to come up with good analogies for these experiences. He decides to test his skill at creating metaphors by relating a state of consciousness he knows well, having dwelt in it often in meditation over the years, one which he knows is not liberated consciousness but close enough to fool even the most adept meditation master.

Dhira says, "In the mountain villages, it gets very cold at night. The snow melting on the rooftops forms icicles on the lintels. One does not see this happening. My mind awake and yet unaware of itself, like those icicles, freezes for a short while, eventually melting, returning to movement, to how it was like before. It is unlike how a boulder rolls down a hillside to rest for eons to come. Tell me, do you know this mind-state I speak of?"

With a burst of energy animating his body, Asanga says, "It is entering the quiescent mind. You move into it, stay there quietly, and then emerge from it back into thought."

Dhira considers Asanga's response and then turns his attention to Buddhi, who has been standing in silence with her eyes closed. They wait for her to open her eyes. Where her mind has gone, they do not know, but her face shines smooth and still.

She eventually opens her eyes and says, "I do not recall the mind-state you speak of. I have just returned from a mind-state more like when a boulder rolls down a hill to rest for eons than one that freezes and melts."

"Then you have known this mind-state," Dhira says. "It is a precursor to the mind-state you have just experienced."

"Then, it is a temporary stillness situated between periods of thought. It eventually leads to an even greater stillness, one that appears to last forever."

"That is right," Dhira says.

"She said what I said," Asanga says.

"But," she says, "I did not hear what you said."

"That is right too," Dhira says, "for she could not have heard you in the mind-state she was in."

"I am not sure of that," Asanga says.

"I am," Buddhi says.

Dhira cannot help but notice how they antagonize each other. But he cannot say anything about it. For he knows, by how they talk about their meditative experiences, that both of them believe themselves to be beyond something as grossly human as envy. If they will not look at their envious thoughts and competitive behavior, then he, their teacher, will have to initiate an investigation in that area.

Dhira says, "Tell me, what is the source conflict, pride, and slander?"

Asanga and Buddhi go back to their separate huts to ponder this question. They each take a different approach.

Buddhi sits in meditation going over in her mind instances of conflict, pride, and slander. She sits with her memories, tears streaming down her cheeks as she recalls one conflict after another. But she soon discovers that slander is difficult to recollect, since she cannot recall ever speaking ill of another person.

Asanga ponders the question abstractly. He knows that the source of conflict must lie underneath the pride someone has in his views. But slander is something that he cannot see within himself because he still thinks ill of others. There are teachers from other sects who hold wrong views and deceive their students. How could he not criticize them? To sit by and do nothing would be agreeing with their erroneous views. He must point out the flaws in their thinking and engage them in debate. When he sits with this predicament, it occurs to him that the source of slander is the absence of conflict over his pride.

Buddhi takes a different path once she becomes aware that she does not know her own acts of slander. She recalls how she felt when the village boys teased her because she recited holy verses, and how her brothers looked down on her just because she was a girl. Then she feels her father's rage at her for learning faster than her brothers. Spreading slander is ignorance. She sees her whole family as incredibly cruel and stupid. Slandering is a stupid, cruel way of behaving. It is not suitable for anyone embarking on the path to liberation. It is made up of spite, shame, and pride, and it is as offensive as excrement.

Still, she has not gone far enough, for she feels the spiteful embers of slander burning in her heart. She asks herself who she has spoken ill of recently. Only then does she realize that she has hated Asanga since they first met. She considers him an arrogant fool. There she sees her pride. She competes with him for Dhira's attention and praise. There she sniffs out her envy. Asanga is no different than one of her brothers. She then sees how she has been reliving the whole situation with her father and eldest brother these past few days with Dhira and Asanga. But the reality is that Dhira has treated her as Asanga's equal, so she should have no fear of Asanga changing Dhira's opinion of her. Dhira is not her father and is Asanga is not Arjuna. They are both intelligent and compassionate men.

The next day, Dhira, Asanga, and Buddhi meet before going on alms round. Dhira repeats the question as to the source of conflict, pride, and slander, and then waits for their responses.

Buddhi's face tears up.

She says, "I must seek compassion from Venerable Asanga. I thought ill of him because I was afraid he would win Dhira over. Then I imagined I would lose Dhira's favor and be cast out. But I know that is not true. It is just my past frightening me again."

Asanga is drawn into her depth of genuine self-knowledge and so speaks from his heart, his voice trembling.

"Young Sister, I know that I am argumentative, competitive, and arrogant. Because I must always be the victor, I have not given you your due respect."

Then, in a rare gesture for a bhikshu, Asanga kneels on the ground in front of Buddhi, bowing three times in a display of sincere reverence.

Through such actions Dhira knows they have understood what he asked them to investigate. Now, he can describe meditative states to them and they will become more interested in exploring what the mind experiences in meditation than in arguing over who has the right interpretation.

XVII

A week later, the three of them meet inadvertently at the house of the village chieftain. It is not a proper situation for them to talk, so they decide to meet again at Dhira's temple in the afternoon. After the meal, however, Venerable Dhira is asked to speak to all those assembled. He addresses about thirty people in the mango grove adjacent to the chieftain's house. A cool breeze stirs the trees and refreshes those gathered, buoying them awake after the big meal.

"We live in an age of confusion over the truth of the Buddha's teaching. Some say that the original teaching is limited and inferior because it pertains only to those inclined to follow the path leading to nirvana. It is a selfish path, one that only bhikshus can aspire to. It is a solitary path, not for those who live in the world. It is an arrogant path, for it places the person who is on it above those who are not. And yet it was taught as the true path to liberation.

"Was the Buddha mistaken in teaching only this path in the beginning? For surely, he knew the path he had taken, the path of sacrifice for all living beings, was a good path too. His path was not selfish, for it included the liberation of others along with his own. It was not solitary, since he taught those who were close to him, and those who traveled a great distance to hear his teaching. It did not foster arrogance in him as it does for those who now say they walk that very same path. With all these flaws out in the open, why did the Buddha not teach the Bodhisattva Path? Why did he teach the inferior Arhat Path instead?

"I cannot begin to understand the motivations of a fully awakened being, but I must conclude that for his age, Gautama's teaching was the right teaching. But now, it is time for the new teaching, the one the Buddha prophesied as the Dharma that will replace his.

"That is the Dharma of Maitreya, the next Buddha, who will teach us how to work on our own liberation and the liberation of others at the same time. This will be a path of working together, practicing together, and realizing liberation together. It shall not be a solitary path. Those who walk it will be joined together on it. From one lifetime to another we have been cultivating the perfections of mind that lead to all of us becoming Buddhas. It is the path of friendship over the ages, dispelling the clouds of ignorance. That is what Maitreya's Dharma will bring to all of us."

His listeners smile, basking in his words, touching a pillar of confidence in the Bodhisattva Path. Asanga, in particular, is uplifted by these lofty and grand ideals.

Now that they are at Dhira's temple, Dhira describes another meditation experience.

"It is like entering a cool lake in the hot season. You swim underwater and see a chest with glittering jewels sunk in the sandy bottom. A exhilarating pleasure flows through your body and you desire to bring the chest back up to the surface. You swim toward the glittering jewels and grab the chest with both hands, but it will not budge. Running out of air, you then swim back to the surface. After a few breaths, you go back underwater and attempt to find the chest again. But it has disappeared. Instead, something else is there, such as a gold disk partially submerged in the sand. It now catches your eye and you swim toward it. You attempt to pull it free, but once again you fail to dislodge it, even though it is small and light. You return to the surface empty-handed. Do you know this mind-state?"

"It is the first *dhyana*," Asanga states.

"How is it like the first dhyana?" Dhira says.

"There is movement, swimming. There is absorption on an object, the jewels in the chest. Pleasure flows through the whole body. That is *priti*. Your breathing stops, just as it does underwater. When you return to this realm of existence, your breathing becomes rapid, saturating your body with bliss."

"That is a very precise description," Dhira says. "What do you have to say, Buddhi?"

Buddhi takes her time answering. Asanga's description sounds plausible to her as well. She begins to doubt her own interpretation. She fears being wrong and observes how that fear tears down her confidence.

She says, "The swimmer goes down to the chest of jewels and tries to lift it, but it will not move. The chest of jewels is a representation of the immovable. It is not nirvana, but from seeing it, and from touching it, you know something about nirvana, though words cannot be put to it. That it changes its representation to something else on the second dive describes how your mind keeps making concepts about nirvana. What we then bring back to the surface with us is not nirvana, but the memory of a concept of nirvana. Deep within us, however, we may know something nonconceptual about nirvana from having caught a brief glimpse of it."

"I do not understand how you have come to that interpretation," Asanga says. "It is clearly the first dhyana."

Buddhi says, "The Buddha stated that one can know nirvana from the first dhyana. Perhaps this is how it happens."

"So, you are saying that the sign of the dhyana is a representation of nirvana?" Asanga says. "That sounds deluded to me."

Buddhi pauses a moment to think. She is well aware that the sign of a dhyana cannot be a representation of nirvana, and though she hates to admit it, to state such a view is deluded.

"You are right, Asanga. It is foolish of me to propose that the sign of the first dhyana would impart knowledge of nirvana. That is an error found in other teachings. I must confess that I think you are right. This is the first dhyana and nothing more."

Asanga is pleased by her admission. Now they are on equal footing. She is no longer the prized student. They both are.

Dhira chooses his words carefully.

"The tendency to come to a definite conclusion about a mind-state can stop you from exploring its unknown depths."

Dhira then walks away, leaving them to their own thoughts. Asanga and Buddhi are silent for a long time. Neither of them is comfortable speaking to the other without Dhira present. Asanga experiences the discomfort as tension in his throat and chest. Buddhi does not know what to say and so vacillates between saying nothing and chanting something. But if she decides to chant something, it has to be something profound and not something devotional, so she goes through what she has committed to heart, and then begins to chant these verses:

> *"If something has an essence—*
> *How can it ever change*
> *Into anything else?*
> *A thing does not change into something else—*
> *Youth does not age,*
> *Age does not age.*
> *If something changed into something else—*
> *Milk would be butter*
> *Or butter would not be milk.*
> *Were there a trace of something,*
> *There would be a trace of emptiness.*
> *Were there no trace of anything,*
> *There would be no trace of emptiness.*
> *Buddhas say emptiness*
> *Is relinquishing opinions.*
> *Believers in emptiness*
> *Are incurable."*

Asanga listens to her sweet voice transport him beyond the words, where he contemplates the wisdom of the enlightened philosopher, Nagarjuna, the originator of these verses.

Asanga says, "Nagarjuna questions the idea that there is an unchanging essence beneath this world of change. Yet he hints at the possibility that emptiness is the essence of all things."

Buddhi says, "What if he the truly saw emptiness in all things?"

"Then emptiness would be found in both nirvana and samsara. Is that what you are saying?"

Buddhi replies, "As the enlightened philosopher says, 'Emptiness is the relinquishing of opinions.'"

Asanga takes her comment as a rebuke. It stings.

He says, "You see me as being attached to my opinions, but you are the incurable believer in emptiness."

Buddhi regrets reciting these verses, meant only to break the tension and not add to it. Now she is anxious about how Asanga may interpret anything she will say in his current state of mind.

She says, "We are both seeking a cure."

"That we agree on."

Buddhi sits with her eyes closed in meditation, while Asanga sits with his eyes open in earnest thought. He goes over a story about himself, one that he wishes to tell her, so that she may know who he truly is and let go of the opinion she has of him.

"I do not know if you can hear me, even though I am sitting close to you," he says, trying to see if his words register a response on her face. There is none. He tells her anyway.

"I live at the doorway to nirvana. I cannot go in. Most of the time, the door is solid and impenetrable, though there are moments when it is as clear as glass and as porous as a sponge. That is when I can intuit the emptiness of the other side. It is not the essence Nagarjuna speaks of, but rather, the world on my side of the door is somehow less substantial, less self-driven, less bound by the laws of samsara. In this way, for me, emptiness is in samsara as much as it is of nirvana. This is not merely a concept. It is a knowledge that lives inside of me."

Buddhi remains in meditation. Asanga's words may not have penetrated. He waits a few minutes to see what will happen next. She emerges and recites these verses:

"The dharma taught by buddhas
Hinges on two truths:
Partial truths of the world
And truths which are sublime.
Without knowing how they differ,
You cannot know the deep;
Without relying on conventions,
You cannot disclose the sublime;
Without intuiting the sublime,
You cannot experience freedom."

Asanga feels a swell of joy at her having chosen these verses to recite. He knows she has heard him, and that this is where they both agree. What is seen as incompatible for the path of liberation is also part of the path of liberation. Knowing your own mind and knowing the Dharma differ, and yet freedom from suffering is not found knowing one without the other.

He wishes to communicate this to Buddhi, but when he looks at her, he can tell that she has returned to the emptiness within her. It is time for them to part ways for the day.

XVIII

Asanga and Buddhi continue to meet alone for several weeks. Buddhi recites verses while Asanga ponders them. He then communicates his thoughts to her as she sits in meditation. When she emerges from meditation, she recites another verse related in some intuitive way to Asanga's ideas. All of Buddhi's verses have been recollections of teachings she has memorized; but then, unexpectedly, she produces an original verse. Asanga is both perplexed and astonished by her creation. He must tell Dhira.

"Recite this extraordinary verse," Dhira says.

"There is the imagination (he).
Duality is not found in him,
But emptiness (she) is.
He is found in her."

Dhira says, "What is meant by 'He is found in her'?"

Asanga replies, "Imagination is found in emptiness! It is the nondual nature of nirvana."

"But it sounds to me as though samsara is nondual as well. If the imagination can be found in emptiness, and they both are truly nondual, then emptiness can be found in the world of the imagination."

"Then there would be no difference between nirvana and samsara," Asanga says. "But perhaps there is a more obvious meaning."

Asanga paces back and forth, thinking to himself, and then he stops pacing and says, "Buddhi speaks these verses from a deep meditative state. While she is in that state, I sit nearby and speak my thoughts. Moments later, she recites verses that illuminate those ideas. In the past, all the verses were ones she had memorized, but today she recited a new verse of our own creation. I am the imagination. She is the emptiness. My mind enters the empty state of her mind. From the emptiness that is her, my ideas reappear in a purified form."

"Is it then not her who speaks?" Dhira says.

"It is her and it is not her, both," Asanga says.

"Who are you in this?"

"I am the thinker of the thoughts and the receiver of the understandings. There is no duality in this dialog. What emerges is not mine, not hers, but ours and everyone's."

"Is this the Dharma of the Buddha?" Dhira asks skeptically.

Asanga is drawn into himself, his energy deflated. He does not know if it is. It is too new to call It, "The Dharma." But in his heart that is exactly what he feels It must be.

Months pass with each new day bringing several new verses as both Asanga and Dhira now feed their ideas into Buddhi's meditative emptiness. A collection of teachings starts to take shape in this way. After they recite the new verses at the end of the day, they see what they now need to know and decide what ideas to introduce next. The verses cover a variety of subjects, staying towards the middle between the extremes of *it is* and *it is not*.

Before they have a chance to analyze these new teachings, Asanga wishes to carry these verses into the world. That is when Asanga and Buddhi have their conversation about spreading the Dharma. Asanga strongly believes that he now possesses the true Dharma of the next Buddha, so he decides to attribute these new teachings to Maitreya. But he purposely neglects to tell Buddhi and Dhira that.

During Asanga's last night of his twelve years in the forest, he has a memorable dream. The dream begins with him on alms round. He stops beneath a banyan tree to eat his food. There is nothing unusual as he eats his meal, except this time he listens to the rustling of the leaves as he chews. Then, as he peers into his alms bowl, he sees maggots crawling on his hand. The maggots crawl up his arms and cover his whole body. He closes his eyes and then lies down on the hard tree roots. The maggots burrow into his flesh. The pain gets so severe he passes out.

When he comes to, he finds himself in the arms of a giant Buddha, who is freeing the maggots with Her tongue, gently setting them down on the ground. With his body free of the maggots, Asanga turns into a dog, who then walks behind Her, waging his tail, smiling up at his savior. The female Buddha leads the dog down a dirt road and into a bustling village. When the villagers approach the dog, the female Buddha introduces him as Asanga. But none of them are able to see Asanga, except for a hundred-year-old woman. Asanga is dismayed that he can only be seen by her and not anyone else. All they see is a dog being led by an enlightened bhikshuni, who, as he focuses on her face, is Buddhi. And with that realization, he wakes up from the dream.

On the morning of Asanga's departure, while she is meditating, Buddhi enters into a realm of expansive white light. She strives to see to the horizon of the light. As her mind travels there, she peers down into each of the worlds she hovers above, noticing the people below. She does not recognize any of their faces, but she knows each of them in their private suffering. Some of the people argue and fight, while others pursue love and are surrounded by children, and then are those who are alone. She is happy to be above them in the sky, untethered. But that does not last long. Her aerial vision zooms in on a girl of ten who has been told by her father that she must marry a cruel brahmin boy.

Buddhi's mind falls into the girl's body. She looks around her and now recognizes all of their faces. She knows them as her extended bodhisattva family. As their future Buddha, she will remain tethered to each one of them throughout their journey in samsara. She vows not to enter nirvana before them. But, she will have to learn the Arhat Path backwards and forwards, so whenever they stray from It, she can lead them back to It.

That is her Bodhisattva Path.

XIX

Sixteen years later, Asanga returns. The teachings of Maitreya have become popular and many prominent bhikshus have requested more advanced teachings on the Bodhisattva Path. Asanga knows he cannot write such teachings alone.

When he arrives at Dhira's home monastery, he learns that Dhira left his human body and now resides in Tushita. Asanga stays up past midnight chanting the verses of Maitreya, hoping that Dhira might hear them and visit Asanga in a dream. But, alas, Asanga enjoys the emptiness of deep sleep.

That morning, Asanga sets out to visit Buddhi. She still lives in the same hut. They sit on the log near the road. She is polite, but then brutally honest.

"What you have done with our teachings is not appropriate."

"I have only made them popular."

"That is not what saddens me," Buddhi says.

"What does then?"

"You attributed our verses to Maitreya. Why did you not tell everyone the true story?"

"I will let my brother Vasubandhu do that. He is the truth-seeker of the family. I am the myth-maker."

Asanga pauses for a moment, catching her smile briefly, and says, "And, you are the source of bodhisattva wisdom. You are truly Maitreya!"

"No, Asanga, I am not Maitreya! I don't know what led you to believe that I was."

Buddhi feels uncomfortable at the thought of anyone discovering that she is one of the creators of the myth of Maitreya. All she wanted to do was produce a profound Dharma teaching for her own edification? And Asanga and Dhira helped her put It into words.

Just at that moment, as if Asanga can hear her thoughts, he says, "Wisdom can be found in myth and fiction. But that does not excuse my intentional deceptions."

"Nor mine," she says.

"How have you deceived?"

"By speaking knowingly of the Dharma when I was only just getting to know what the Dharma is."

"We are all guilty of that," Asanga says. "But now we know what the Dharma is."

"How do *you* know that for sure?"

"Because some very wise people, including my brother, Vasubandhu, have been studying Maitreya's teachings for many years now. They can see the true Dharma in those teachings. Without our teachings, there may be no field of investigation for that wisdom to arise."

Buddhi says, "I do not believe that to be so. The Dharma is inside each of us, waiting to be discovered."

"For you, yes, that is so," Asanga says. "But in our current age, most people need a set of teachings outside of themselves in order to find the Dharma within. And that is where you come in."

Buddhi is surprised at herself for it taking so long to realize why Asanga has returned. It is all too obvious.

"You want me to help you craft some new teachings."

"You understand me perfectly," Asanga says. "Now, there is something we have left unsaid."

"What is that?"

"The story of how a bodhisattva goes from one existence to another, cultivating the perfections of a Buddha, never ceasing until all the beings enter nirvana."

"But that is yet to be known."

"Why should that stop us?" Asanga says. "If our Bodhisattva Path sounds plausible, does it matter if It is not yet real?"

Buddhi says, "For me, It has always been real."

"That is what makes you Maitreya!"

Thank you for reading these three Buddhist tales. If you would like to explore these stories further, I will have extra material linked to my website:

https://jasonsiff.com

I also enjoy hearing from readers, so here is my email address:

jasonsiff@gmail.com

CPSIA information can be obtained
at www.ICGtesting.com
Printed in the USA
BVHW031426271221
624937BV00007B/363